ADOBE® SOUNDBOOTH™

P9-CDC-020

CLASSROOM IN A BOOK®

The official training workbook from Adobe Systems

Adobe

Contents

Getting Started

1 A Quick Tour of Adobe Soundbooth

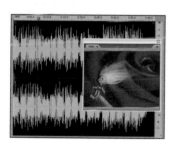

2 Understanding the Basics of Digital Audio

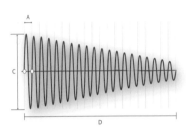

3 Navigating the Workspace

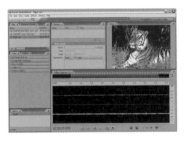

4   Repairing and Adjusting Audio Clips

5   Editing and Enhancing Voiceover Recordings

6   Creating Background Music

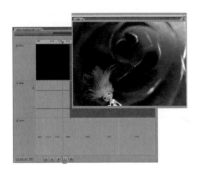

7   Exploring Effects

8   Working with Markers

9   Importing, Exporting, and Round-trip Editing

Lesson files . . . and so much more

The *Adobe Soundbooth CS3 Classroom in a Book* CD includes the lesson files that you'll need to complete the exercises in this book, as well as other content to help you learn more about Adobe Soundbooth and use it with greater efficiency and ease. The diagram below represents the contents of the CD, which should help you locate the files you need.

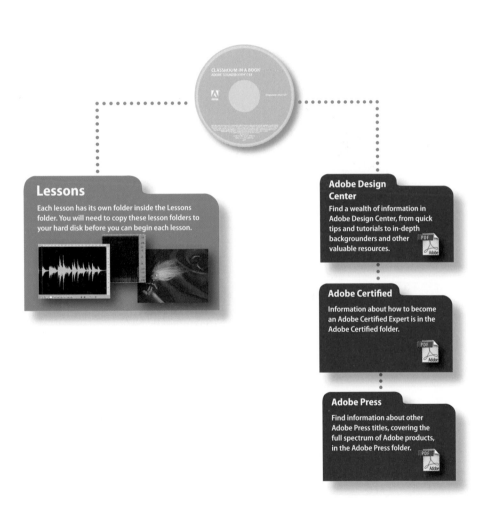

Lessons

Each lesson has its own folder inside the Lessons folder. You will need to copy these lesson folders to your hard disk before you can begin each lesson.

Adobe Design Center

Find a wealth of information in Adobe Design Center, from quick tips and tutorials to in-depth backgrounders and other valuable resources.

Adobe Certified

Information about how to become an Adobe Certified Expert is in the Adobe Certified folder.

Adobe Press

Find information about other Adobe Press titles, covering the full spectrum of Adobe products, in the Adobe Press folder.

Getting Started

Adobe® Soundbooth® CS3 enables you to edit and create audio with fast, intuitive tools. Take command of your audio in film, video, and Adobe Flash® software projects with task-based tools to clean up recordings, polish voiceovers, customize music and sound effects, and much more. Adobe Soundbooth CS3 software has an intuitive interface that helps you get the job done quickly without sacrificing creative control.

Soundbooth CS3 is ideal for professional audio/video producers, corporate and event videographers, Web designers, and Flash professionals, who will enjoy the tight integration between the programs.

In this *Adobe Soundbooth CS3 Classroom in a Book,* you'll learn the fundamental concepts and techniques that help you master the application.

About Classroom in a Book

Adobe Soundbooth CS3 Classroom in a Book is part of the official training series for Adobe graphics and publishing software developed by Adobe product experts. Each lesson in this book is made up of a series of self-paced projects that give you hands-on experience using Soundbooth CS3.

The *Adobe Soundbooth CS3 Classroom in a Book* includes a CD attached to the inside back cover of this book. On the CD you'll find all the files used for the lessons in this book, along with additional learning resources.

Prerequisites

Before beginning to use *Adobe Soundbooth CS3 Classroom in a Book,* you should have a working knowledge of your computer and its operating system. Make sure you know how to use the mouse and standard menus and commands, and how to open, save, and close files. If you need to review these techniques, see the printed or online documentation relating to your Windows or Mac OS systems.

Note: The lessons in this book are designed to be used on either Microsoft® Windows XP, Windows Vista, or Mac OS X v.10.4.9 with Intel® processor.

Requirements on your computer

You'll need about 500 MB of free space on your hard disk for the lesson files and the work files you'll create. The lesson files necessary for your work in this book are on the CD attached to the inside back cover of this book.

Installing the program

Before you begin using *Adobe Soundbooth CS3 Classroom in a Book,* make sure your system is set up correctly and that you've installed the required software and hardware. You must purchase the Adobe Soundbooth CS3 software separately and install it on your computer. For system requirements and complete instructions on installing the software, see the "How to Install" Readme file on the application CD.

Copying the Classroom in a Book files

The CD attached to the inside back cover of this book includes a Lessons folder containing all the electronic files for the lessons in this book. You must install these folders on your hard disk to use the files for the lessons. Keep all the lesson files on your computer until after you have finished all the lessons.

Note: The digital files on the CD are practice files, provided for your personal use in these lessons. You are not authorized to use these files commercially, or to publish or distribute them in any form without written permission from Adobe Systems, Inc. and the individuals who created them, or other copyright holders.

1 Insert the *Adobe Soundbooth CS3 Classroom in a Book* CD into your CD-ROM drive. If a message appears asking what you want Windows to do, select Open Folder to View Files Using Windows Explorer, and click OK. If no message appears, open My Computer and double-click the CD icon to open it.

2 Browse the CD contents and locate the Lessons folder.

3 Do one of the following:

• To copy all of the lessons, drag the Lessons folder from the CD onto your hard disk.

• To copy only the individual lessons, first create a new folder on your hard disk and name it **Lessons**. Then, drag the lesson folder or folders that you want to copy from the CD into the Lessons folder on your hard disk.

Note: As you complete each lesson, you might overwrite the start files. If you want to restore the original files, recopy the corresponding lesson folder from the Adobe Soundbooth CS3 Classroom in a Book CD to the Lessons folder on your hard disk.

Additional resources

Adobe Soundbooth CS3 Classroom in a Book is not meant to replace documentation that comes with the program, nor is it designed to be a comprehensive reference for every feature in Adobe Soundbooth CS3. For additional information about program features, refer to any of these resources:

• Soundbooth Help, which is built into the Adobe Soundbooth CS3 application. You can view it by choosing Help > Soundbooth Help.

• The Adobe Web site (http://www.adobe.com), which you can view by choosing Help > Soundbooth Online. You can also choose Help > Online Support for access to the support pages on the Adobe Web site. Both of these options require that you have Internet access.

• The Adobe Soundbooth CS3 Getting Started Guide, which is included either in the box with your copy of Adobe Soundbooth, or on the installation CD for the application software in PDF format. If you don't already have Adobe Reader (or if you have an older version of Adobe Acrobat Reader) installed on your computer, you can download a free copy from the Adobe Web site (http://www.adobe.com).

Adobe Certification

The Adobe Training and Certification Programs are designed to help Adobe customers improve and promote their product-proficiency skills. The Adobe Certified Expert (ACE) program is designed to recognize the high-level skills of expert users. Adobe Certified Training Providers (ACTP) use only Adobe Certified Experts to teach Adobe software classes. Available in either ACTP classrooms or on-site, the ACE program is the best way to master Adobe products. For Adobe Certified Training Programs information, visit the Partnering with Adobe Web site at http://partners.adobe.com.

Whether you want to repair audio clips, enhance voiceover recordings, apply effects, or create loops and scores, Adobe Soundbooth CS3 makes it possible to get professional results with ease.

1 | A Quick Tour of Adobe Soundbooth

In this lesson, you will be introduced to the tools and the interface of Adobe Soundbooth CS3. Future lessons provide more in-depth exercises and specific details of the tools and features.

To give you a quick overview of Soundbooth's capabilities, you will listen to audio samples as they sound before and after being processed. The tools used in the processing of the samples are briefly explained, but for now you don't have to actually perform the editing tasks. Step-by-step instructions on how to use the tools are provided in the remaining lessons.

In this lesson, you'll work on removing noise and other recording artifacts from audio files, visually editing sound in waveform and spectral frequency displays, recording and enhancing voiceovers, creating customized background music, adding markers and exporting them for use in Flash projects, using Help, and accessing additional resources on the internet.

Before you begin, make sure that you have correctly copied the Lessons folder from the CD in the back of this book onto your computer's hard disk. See "Copying the Classroom in a Book files" on page 2.

Getting started

Perform the following steps to ensure that you start the lesson with the default window layout.

1   Start Adobe Soundbooth.

2   Select Window > Workspace > Default, if it is not already selected. Then, choose Window > Workspace > Reset "Default."

3   In the Reset Workspace dialog box, click OK.

Cleaning-up audio

Audio recordings frequently contain flaws such as hisses, hums, rumbling, crackling, pops, or other unwanted background noise. Soundbooth offers task-based tools that enable you to quickly repair such recordings.

Removing clicks and pops

Dust and scratches on old vinyl records cause audio clicks and pops when played back or recorded into digital format. To listen to a typical example of such a recording, do the following:

1   In Soundbooth, choose File > Open. In the Open Files dialog box that appears, navigate to your Lesson01 folder you copied to your hard disk. Within that folder, select the file Vinyl_01_Before.wav, and then click Open.

Note: *If you don't see the file, choose All Supported Media from the Files of type menu.*

The Import Files dialog box will appear briefly while the sound file is opened. Once open, the file is listed in the Files panel and its waveform is displayed in the Editor panel.

If the Editor panel looks different on your computer than in the illustration on the next page, you might need to turn off the menu option View > Spectral Frequency Display. You will learn more about the Spectral Frequency Display view of the Editor panel in Lesson 3, "Getting to know the Workspace," and in Lesson 4, "Repairing and Adjusting Audio Clips."

2   To listen to the sound file you just opened, click the Play button () located at the bottom of the Editor panel.

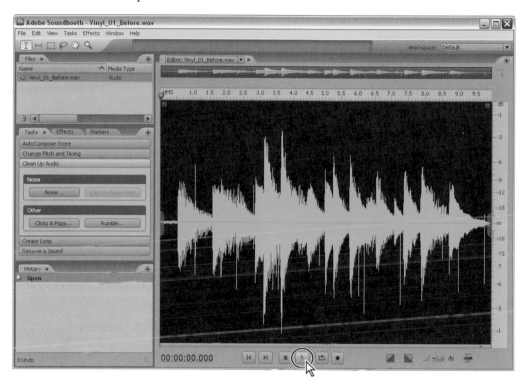

You can clearly hear the clicks and pops stemming from dust and scratches in the groove of the old vinyl record. In the Editor panel, you can recognize the clicks and pops by the sharp spikes in the waveform. You can eliminate these flaws from the recording using Soundbooth's Clicks & Pops tool. You can specify the tool's sensitivity to audio artifacts in the Clicks & Pops dialog box. To help you while adjusting the settings for best-sounding results, you can preview the processed audio and compare it with the original version, before clicking OK to actually process the file.

Removing noise

The recording also suffers from noise. This noise is clearly visible at the beginning of the file, before any instruments have begun playing. If you listen carefully, you can notice the noise throughout the recording.

Removing background noise in Soundbooth is a one- or two-step task. Ideally, you can identify a section in your recording that contains nothing but the noise you want to eliminate. For example, look at the beginning of the file Vinyl_01_Before.wav. This section of blank audio can be used as a *noise print* for the entire audio file. Soundbooth can use such a noise print to improve the results you can achieve when performing the Clean Up Audio Noise task. In the Noise dialog box, you specify the aggressiveness of the tool as well as the amount of noise to remove. As in the Clicks & Pops dialog box, you can preview the processed audio and compare it with the original version before clicking OK to actually process the file.

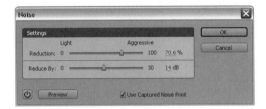

After processing is complete, the changes are clearly visible in the waveform display. Gone are the spikes, as well as the noise that was visible at the beginning of the file.

To confirm that the cleaned-up sound file not only looks better in the waveform display but also sounds better, do the following:

1   Choose File > Open. In the Open Files dialog box, select in the Lesson01 folder the file Vinyl_01_After.wav, and then click Open.

2   Click the Play button (▶) in the Editor panel to start playback.

3   To compare the result with the unprocessed version, you can switch back and forth between the files using the files menu located in the top left corner of the Editor panel.

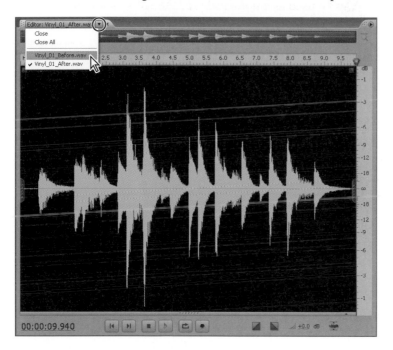

💡 *Usually the last step when cleaning up a sound file is to normalize its volume. Normalizing—a one-click operation in Soundbooth via the Make Louder button— proportionally increases the volume as much as possible without clipping the peak levels.*

Visually editing sound

Once the noise has been removed, you're ready for some editing tasks, like deleting or silencing unwanted sections, trimming the ends, or adding fades. Soundbooth provides intuitive on-clip controls for all of these most commonly performed sound-editing tasks. Finally, using the spectral frequency display, you can visually identify—and easily remove—unwanted background sounds.

Silencing or deleting selections

You can quickly change volume levels of selected audio by using the volume pop-up bubble. Dragging all the way to the left would silence the selection. To delete a selection and have the remaining audio move to the left to close the gap, simply press the delete key on your keyboard. Or, use the familiar cut, copy and paste commands to edit the waveform as you would edit a text document.

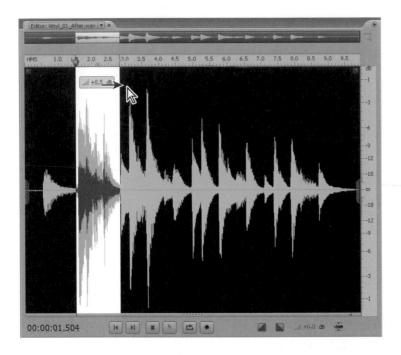

💡 *Click and drag using the Time Selection tool to make a selection in the waveform display. Double-click anywhere in the waveform display, or choose Edit > Select View to select the currently visible portion of the file. Triple-click, or choose Edit > Select All to select the entire file. Click once anywhere in the waveform display to clear the current selection.*

Trimming audio

Use the trim handles located at the left and right ends of the waveform, to quickly remove unwanted sections from the beginning or end of the file.

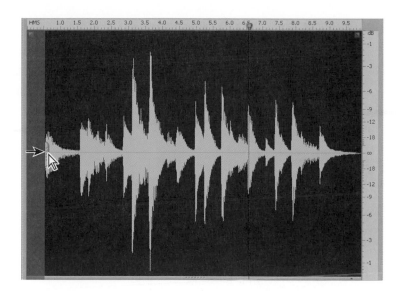

Applying fades

Apply fades by using the Fade In and Fade Out handles. Change the duration of the fade by dragging left or right, or change the characteristic of the fade—linear, exponential, or logarithmic—by dragging up or down.

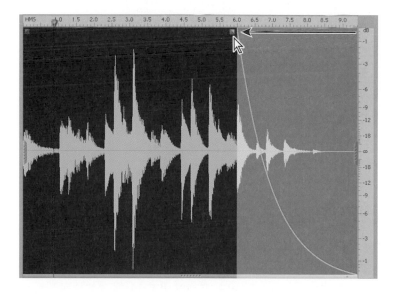

Removing background sounds

Sometimes an otherwise perfect recording is marred by an unwanted background sound such as a cough or a ringing phone. Soundbooth's spectral frequency display enables you to visually pinpoint such intrusions and remove them from the recording—similar to using the healing brush tool in Photoshop. To listen to a typical example of such a recording and to see what the sound of a phone ringing in the background looks like in the spectral frequency display, do the following:

1   Choose File > Open. In the Open Files dialog box, select in the Lesson01 folder the file PhoneRing_01_Before.wav, and then click Open.

Note: The file PhoneRing_01_Before.wav was recorded in stereo, thus featuring two waveforms—one for each channel—in the waveform display.

2   Click the Play button (⏵) in the Editor panel to start playback. 3 to 4 seconds into the recording, notice the sound of a phone ringing in the background.

3   Choose Tasks > Remove a Sound. The spectral frequency display will appear in the Editor panel, and the Remove a Sound section opens in the Tasks panel.

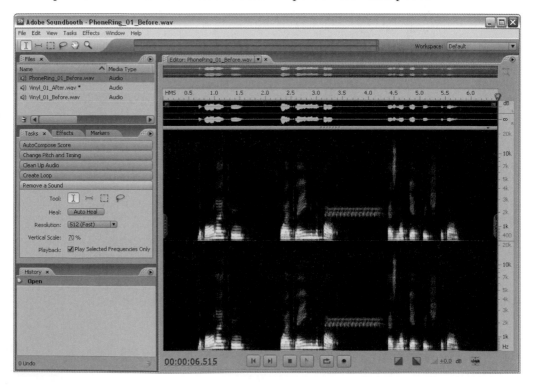

4 Start playback again and watch the current-time indicator (♀) move across the display in the Editor panel. Notice how the sound of the phone ringing coincides with the current-time indicator passing over the bright area in the 2k to 3k frequency range. This is the sound you want to remove from the file.

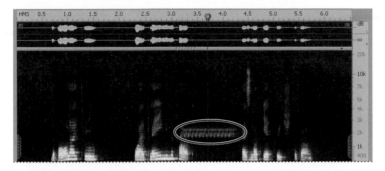

You can select the area of interest in the spectral frequency display by using marquee or lasso selection tools similar to those found in Photoshop. Then, simply silence or delete the selection, leaving a black area indicating the absence of sound in theses frequencies.

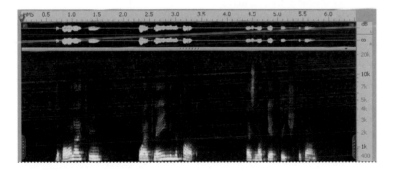

♀ *The Auto Heal command does a better job of removing unwanted sound while leaving desired sound intact by blending the deleted area with the area surrounding it—similar to how the healing brush tool works in Photoshop. However, the selection may not be longer than a certain length (about half a second at a typical sample rate of 44,100 samples per second). This works well for short unwanted sounds like a cough in the background. For sounds with a longer duration, try to remove the sound one piece at a time, using multiple shorter selections.*

5 Open the file PhoneRing_01_After.wav in the Lesson01 folder, and then start playback to listen to the same recording with the sound of the phone ringing removed.

Recording and enhancing voiceovers

You can record sound directly in Soundbooth from a wide range of input devices such as a built-in or external microphone, or a cassette deck, tuner or record player connected to your sound card's Line In port. Next, you can enhance the audio recording by applying effects. Soundbooth offers numerous effect presets for common sound-editing tasks such as enhancing voice recordings or adding special effects like an echo or reverb. These presets are fully customizable if you want to adjust their settings for your special needs.

Recording sound

In the Record dialog box, you can select and configure your input device, as well as choose the sample rate, file location and other recording specific parameters.

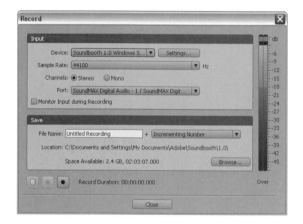

If your speakers are positioned too close to your microphone, using the Monitor Input during Recording option may create a feedback loop resulting in increased noise or squealing sounds while recording. If you can't increase the distance between the speakers and the microphone, e.g. when using a laptop computer with built-in microphone and speakers, you may need to keep this option unchecked.

While recording, you can monitor the sound levels and add markers that can later be exported as Adobe Flash cue points. When done recording, the new file is automatically added to the open files in Soundbooth, ready to be edited.

1 If the spectral frequency display from the previous exercise is still visible in the Editor panel, choose View > Spectral Frequency Display to close it.

2   Choose File > Open. In the Open Files dialog box, select in the Lesson01 folder the file Voiceover_01_Before.wav, and then click Open.

3   Click the Play button (▶) in the Editor panel to listen to the recording.

Changing pitch and timing

To synchronize a voiceover recording with a video scene or web animation, it is often necessary to adjust the length of the recording without noticeably changing the pitch of the voice. Or, perhaps you would like to alter the pitch but keep the length unchanged. Soundbooth lets you adjust the length and pitch of a sound recording independently, using the Change Pitch and Timing task.

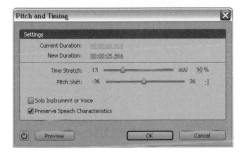

Applying effects

Many of Soundbooth's effect presets are designed for the task of enhancing a voice recording. The Vocal Enhancer effect, while extremely easy to use, can significantly improve the quality of a voiceover recording. Sound levels of certain frequency ranges are adjusted, hissing and popping sounds frequently noticeable in speech are softened, and microphone handling noise is reduced. You have the choice between applying enhancements for a typical female or male voice and toning down background music to better complement a foreground voiceover.

Effects rack presets, such as the Voice: Increase Clarity preset, can combine up to five effects to achieve the desired result.

The user interface of the effect options ranges from being as simple as a single slider to having more advanced options for maximum customizability. For ease of use, each effect comes preconfigured with a wide range of special purpose presets. If necessary, all their settings are also accessible for further fine-tuning.

In addition to effects for the improvement of voice recordings, you will find interesting sound effects—such as delay, chorus, and reverb—that can be applied to any recording, be it a voiceover or music piece.

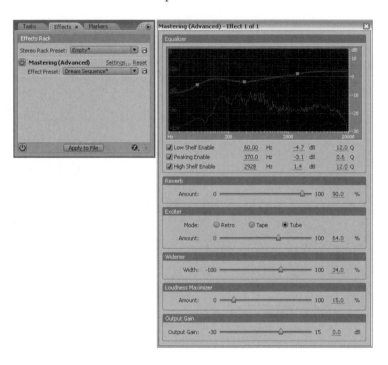

To listen to the same voiceover recording, but with an effect preset applied to it (we used the Dream Sequence effect preset of the Mastering (Advanced) effect), do the following:

1   Choose File > Open. In the Open Files dialog box, select in the Lesson01 folder the file Voiceover_01_After.wav, and then click Open.

2   Click the Play button (▶) in the Editor panel to listen to the recording.

Producing custom music

Apart from letting you record and edit music, Soundbooth also enables you to create you very own background music for use in other projects such as videos or web animations. You can turn a portion of a waveform into a seamless loop, intended to be repeated continuously in your project. Or, create royalty-free custom background music from score templates.

Creating loops

Creating a loop in Soundbooth couldn't be easier. All you have to do is to make a selection in the waveform, set a few options in the Create Loop task panel, and then save the loop in your file format of choice.

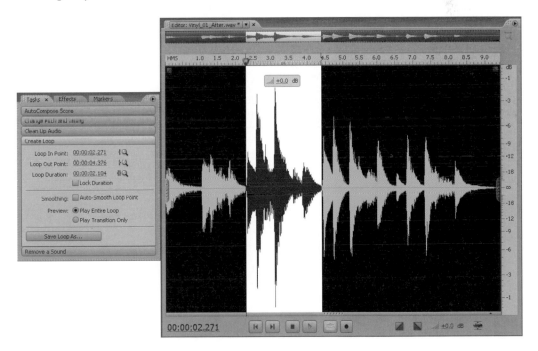

Using scores

With the help of the AutoComposer and customizable score templates you can now create your very own background music for your video projects—without having to be a musician yourself. A score template contains a rich set of audio recordings plus additional metadata to control playback. You can customize the music for your purpose using the AutoCompose Score task. To watch a short movie and listen to the background music created for it using a score template, do the following:

1   Choose File > Open. In the Open Files dialog box, make sure to have either "All Supported Media" or "MPEG Movie (*.mpeg,*.vob,…,*.mp4,…,*.264)" selected in the Files of type (Windows) or Enable (Mac OS) menu.

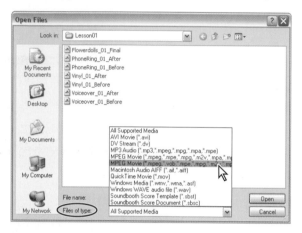

2   Select the file Flowerdolls_01_Final.mp4 in the Lesson01 folder, and then click Open.

3   Wait until the waveform gets loaded and the Video panel opens, and then click the Play button ( ) in the Editor panel to start playback. Notice how well the music supplements the video.

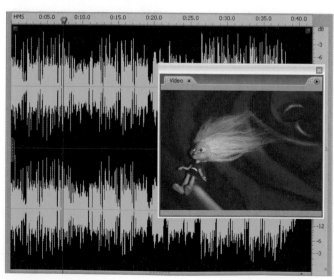

Creating the music for this little video clip takes only a few minutes. First, you load a score template and a reference video clip in the AutoCompose Score task.

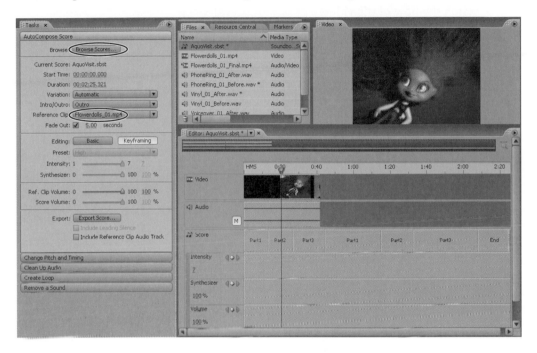

Next, you adjust the length of the score to match the length of the video clip. The AutoComposer will automatically add, remove, lengthen or shorten sections of the score to fit the chosen length.

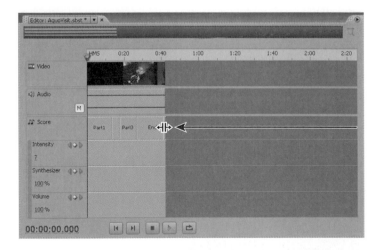

To further customize your creation, choose a preset to vary the overall intensity or other parameters of the score. Add keyframes to adjust these settings over time to perfectly match the flow of the video.

Finally, choose from a variety of file formats to export your score as a sound file or a video clip complete with background music. Soundbooth includes some scores at install time and more scores are available for download from Adobe's Resource Central Web site.

Working with markers

Soundbooth lets you add markers to your sound file to facilitate navigating in the Editor panel, as well as to export them for reuse in a Flash animation or other projects.

Adding and editing markers

You can add markers on the fly while recording a new file, or add them later in the Editor panel. The Markers panel (Window > Markers) provides additional options for working with markers, such as double-clicking a marker to jump to that position in the Editor panel.

Markers can be repositioned easily by dragging them in the timeline of the Editor panel.

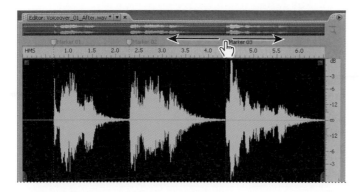

Use the context menu in the Markers panel to remove Markers you no longer need.

Exporting markers for use as Flash cue points

In the Marker Details section, you can add parameter pairs for each marker that can be accessed—after exporting them as XML—by a media player or through ActionScript in Flash to navigate the file, or to trigger an action like displaying a closed caption.

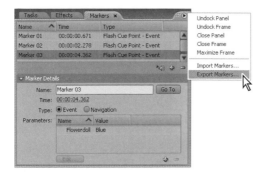

When saving a waveform with markers, the marker data gets written to a separate file from which the marker data is automatically reloaded next time you open that waveform in Soundbooth. Or, you can import the marker data when working with a different waveform to facilitate the synchronization of edit tasks.

Getting help and finding additional resources

Using Help

A great resource for additional information about program features is Soundbooth CS3 Help, accessible via the Help > Adobe Soundbooth Help menu command. The Adobe Help Viewer lets you find information organized by subject and index, or search within the entire help system—even across multiple Adobe applications.

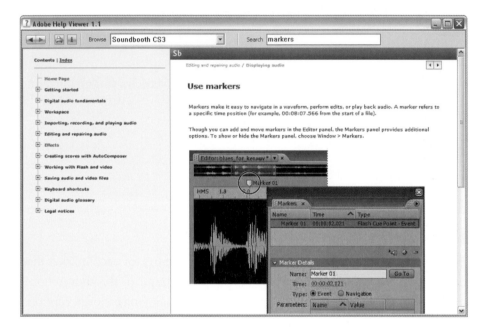

For up-to-date information and links to additional instructional content, visit the Adobe Help Resource center at http://www.adobe.com/go/documentation.

Accessing additional resources

The Resource Central panel (Window > Resource Central) connects you to the latest, dynamically updated content on the Adobe website. There, you'll find extensive collections of sound effects and score templates that increase the power of Soundbooth, as well as expert tips and tutorials that expand your audio knowledge.

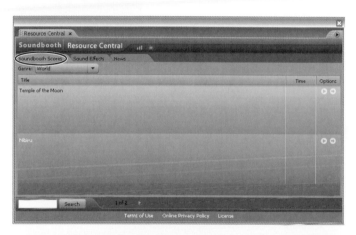

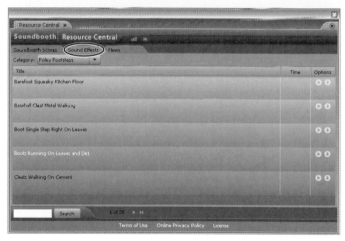

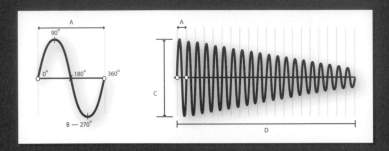

You don't need to be an audio expert to work with Adobe
Soundbooth CS3. However, understanding the basics of
digital audio will help your work sound as good as it looks.

2 | Understanding the Basics of Digital Audio

Comprehending the essential concepts of digital audio and dealing with its terminologies will help your work in Soundbooth.

Understanding sound

Sound waves

Sound starts with vibrations in the air, like those produced by guitar strings, vocal cords, or speaker cones. These vibrations push nearby air molecules together, raising the air pressure slightly. The air molecules under pressure then push on the air molecules surrounding them, which push on the next set of molecules, and so on. As high-pressure areas move through the air, they leave low-pressure areas behind them. When these waves of pressure changes reach us, they vibrate the receptors in our ears, and we hear the vibrations as sound.

When you see a visual waveform that represents audio, it reflects these waves of air pressure. The zero line in the waveform is the pressure of air at rest. When the line rises up to a peak, it represents higher pressure; when the line drops down to a trough, it represents lower pressure.

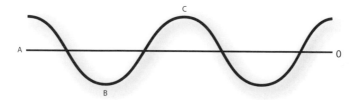

A sound wave represented as a visual waveform.
A. *Zero line.* **B.** *Low-pressure area.* **C.** *High-pressure area.*

Waveform measurements

Several measurements describe sound waveforms:

Amplitude

Reflects the change in pressure from the peak of the waveform to the trough. High-amplitude waveforms are loud; low-amplitude waveforms are quiet.

Cycle

Describes a single, repeated sequence of pressure changes, from zero pressure to high pressure to low pressure and back to zero.

Frequency

Measured in hertz (Hz), describes the number of cycles per second. (For example, a 1000-Hz waveform emits 1000 cycles per second.) The higher the frequency, the higher the musical pitch.

Phase

Measured in 360 degrees, indicates the position of a waveform in a cycle. Zero degrees is the start point, followed by 90° at high pressure, 180° at the halfway point, 270° at low pressure, and 360° at the end point.

Wavelength

Measured in units such as inches or centimeters, is the distance between two points with the same degree phase. As frequency increases, wavelength decreases.

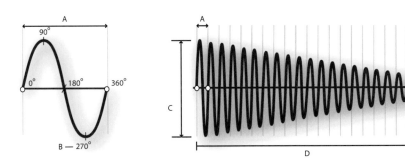

A single cycle at left; a complete, 20-Hz waveform at right.
A. Wavelength. B. Degree of phase. C. Amplitude. D. One second.

How sound waves interact

When two or more sound waves meet, they add to and subtract from each other. If their peaks and troughs are perfectly in phase, they reinforce each other, resulting in a waveform that has higher amplitude than either individual waveform.

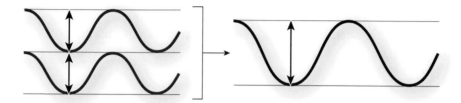

In-phase waves reinforce each other.

If the peaks and troughs of two waveforms are perfectly out of phase, they cancel each other, resulting in no waveform at all.

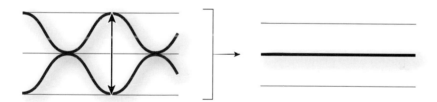

Out-of-phase waves cancel each other.

💡 *Because of its unique physical structure, a single instrument can create extremely complex waves. That's why a violin and a trumpet sound different even when playing the same note.*

In most cases, however, waves are out of phase in varying amounts, resulting in a combined waveform that is more complex than individual waveforms. A complex waveform that represents music, voice, noise, and other sounds, for example, combines the waveform from each sound.

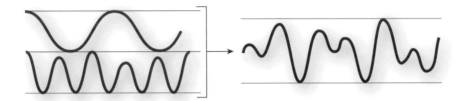

Two simple waves combine to create a complex wave.

Digitizing audio

Comparing analog and digital audio

In analog and digital audio, sound is transmitted and stored in very different ways.

Analog audio: positive and negative voltage

A microphone converts the pressure waves of sound into voltage changes in a wire: high pressure becomes positive voltage, and low pressure becomes negative voltage. When these voltage changes travel down a microphone wire, they can be recorded onto tape as changes in magnetic strength or onto vinyl records as changes in groove size. A speaker works like a microphone in reverse, receiving the voltage signals from an audio recording and vibrating to re-create the pressure wave.

Digital audio: zeroes and ones

Unlike analog storage media such as magnetic tape or vinyl records, computers store audio information digitally as a series of zeroes and ones. In digital storage, the original waveform is broken up into individual snapshots called samples. This process is typically known as digitizing or sampling the audio, but it is sometimes called analog-to-digital conversion.

When you record from a microphone into a computer, for example, analog-to-digital converters transform the analog signal into digital samples that computers can store and process.

Sample rate

Sample rate indicates the number of digital samples taken of an audio signal each second. This rate determines the frequency range of an audio file. The higher the sample rate, the closer the shape of the digital waveform is to that of the original analog waveform. Low sample rates limit the range of frequencies that can be recorded, which can result in a recording that poorly represents the original sound.

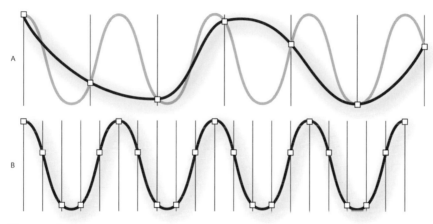

Two sample rates.
*A. Low sample rate that distorts the original sound wave. **B.** High sample rate that perfectly reproduces the original sound wave.*

To reproduce a given frequency, the sample rate must be at least twice that frequency. For example, CDs have a sample rate of 44,100 samples per second, so they can reproduce frequencies up to 22,050 Hz, which is just beyond the limit of human hearing, 20,000 Hz.

Nyquist frequency

The Nyquist frequency, named after Harry Nyquist, is a frequency equal to half the current sample rate, which determines the highest reproducible audio frequency for that rate. This is the reason why this frequency is sometimes referred to as critical frequency. For example, audio CDs use a sample rate of 44,100Hz because the resulting Nyquist frequency is 22,050 Hz—just above the limit of human hearing, 20,000 Hz. For the best audio quality, record and edit at higher sample rates and then convert down if needed.

The following table lists the most common sample rates for digital audio:

Sample rate	Quality level	Frequency range
11,025 Hz	Poor AM radio (low-end multimedia)	0-5,512 Hz
22,050 Hz	New FM radio (high-end multimedia)	0-11,025 Hz
32,000 Hz	Better than FM radio (standard broadcast rate)	0-16,000 Hz
44,100 Hz	CD	0-22,050 Hz
48,000 Hz	Standard DVD	0-24,000 Hz
96,000 Hz	High-end DVD	0-48,000 Hz

Bit depth

Bit depth determines dynamic range. When a sound wave is sampled, each sample is assigned the amplitude value closest to the original wave's amplitude. Higher bit depth provides more possible amplitude values, producing greater dynamic range, a lower noise floor, and higher fidelity.

Bit depth	Quality level	Amplitude values	Dynamic range
8-bit	Telephony	256	48 dB
16-bit	CD	65,536	96 dB
24-bit	DVD	16,777,216	144 dB
32-bit	Best	4,294,967,296	192 dB

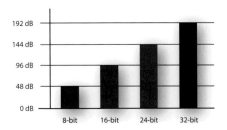

Higher bit depths provide greater dynamic range.

Audio file contents and size

An audio file on your hard disk, such as a WAV file, consists of a small header indicating sample rate and bit depth, and then a long series of numbers, one for each sample. These files can be very large. For example, at 44,100 samples per second and 16 bits per sample, a file requires 86 KB per second—about 5MB per minute. That figure doubles to 10 MB per minute for a stereo CD, which has two channels.

How Soundbooth digitizes audio

When you record audio in Soundbooth, the sound card starts the recording process and specifies what sample rate and bit depth to use. Through Line In or Microphone In ports, the sound card receives analog audio and digitally samples it at the specified rate. Soundbooth stores each sample in sequence until you stop recording.

When you play a file in Soundbooth, the process happens in reverse. Soundbooth sends a series of digital samples to the sound card. The card reconstructs the original waveform and sends it as an analog signal through Line Out ports to your speakers.

To sum up, the process of digitizing audio starts with a pressure wave in the air. A microphone converts this pressure wave into voltage changes. A sound card converts these voltage changes into digital samples. After analog sound becomes digital audio, Soundbooth can record, edit, and process it—the possibilities are limited only by your imagination.

For more information, check out Soundbooth CS3 Help, accessible via the Help > Adobe Soundbooth Help menu command. The Resource Central panel (Window > Resource Central) connects you to the latest, dynamically updated content on the Adobe Web site with expert tips.

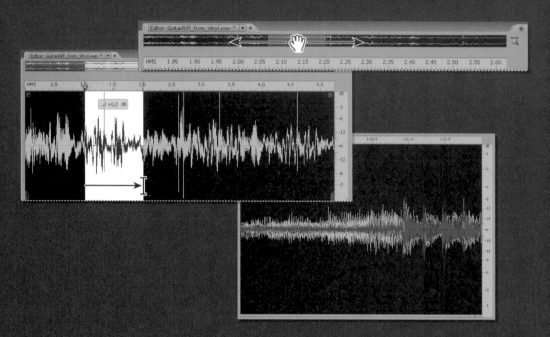

Adobe Soundbooth CS3 software has an intuitive, task-based interface similar to those of other Adobe products. On-clip tools make common edits intuitive, and visual feedback keeps you informed at every step.

3 | Navigating the Workspace

The Soundbooth workspace is made up of a collection of panels, grouping the tools necessary for different aspects of your sound-editing task. If you are familiar with Adobe Premiere Pro or Adobe After Effects, the interface will look familiar. This lesson introduces the various interface items and shows how to customize their arrangement on the screen to suit your preferred working style or requirements.

In this lesson, you will do the following:

- Use the Files panel.

- Work with the Editor panel.

- Select predefined workspaces.

- Customize the layout of your workspace.

Before you begin, make sure that you have correctly copied the Lessons folder from the CD in the back of this book onto your computer's hard disk. See "Copying the Classroom in a Book files" on page 2.

Getting started

Performing the following steps ensures that you start the lesson with the default window layout, and your workspace looks as shown in the illustration below.

1   Start Adobe Soundbooth.

2   Select Window > Workspace > Default, if it is not already selected. Then, choose Window > Workspace > Reset "Default."

3   In the Reset Workspace dialog box, click OK.

Exploring the user interface

When you first launch the Soundbooth application, you will be presented with the main window as shown in the illustration below. The large Editor panel on the right side takes up most of the working area. The Tools panel stretches across the top of the window and on the left side there are various other panels you will learn more about while working through the lessons in this book.

A. Menu bar. B. Tools panel. C. Files panel. D. Editor panel.
E. Panel group containing Tasks panel, Effects panel, and Markers panel. F. History panel.

Note: *The illustration above shows the Windows version of Soundbooth. In Mac OS X, the arrangement is the same, but some of the operating system styles are different (e.g.: In Windows, the menu bar is normally located under the title bar of the application window, while on Mac OS it is anchored at the top of the main screen).*

Opening files

You can use Soundbooth to create new sound files (see Lesson 5, "Editing and Enhancing Voiceover Recordings" and Lesson 6, "Creating Background Music"), or open and edit existing files already stored on your hard disk. Soundbooth understands a variety of audio and video file formats, including AIFF, AVI, MP3, MPEG, QuickTime, WAV, and Windows Media. You will now use different methods to open three files in Soundbooth. We'll start with the Open command.

1   Do one of the following:

- Choose File > Open.

- Use the keyboard shortcut, Ctrl+O (Windows) or Command+O (Mac OS).

- Double-click the Files panel.

Double-clicking the Files panel is a quick way to bring up the Open Files dialog box.
If there are files already listed in the Files panel, make sure to double-click the empty area below the last name.

2   In the Open Files dialog box that appears, navigate to your Lesson03 folder you copied to your hard disk. Within that folder, select the file GuitarRiff_from_Vinyl.wav, and then click Open.

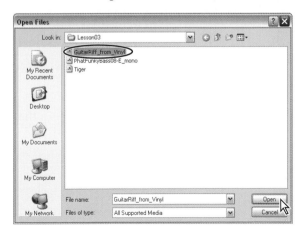

Note: If you don't see the filename or the filename is grayed out, choose All Supported Media from the Files of type (Windows) or Enable (Mac OS) menu.

The Import Files dialog box will appear briefly while the sound file is opened. Once open, the file is listed in the Files panel and its waveform is displayed in the Editor panel.

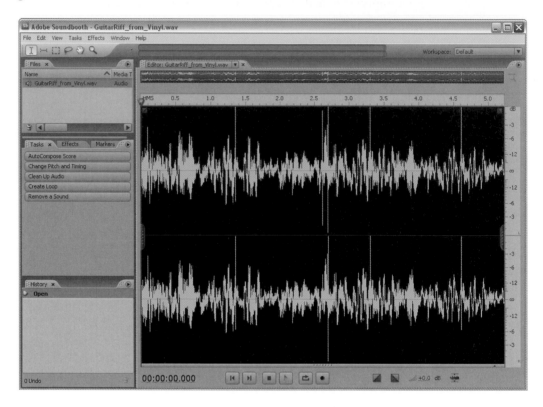

If the Editor panel looks different on your computer than in the illustration above, you might need to turn off the menu option View > Spectral Frequency Display. You will learn more about the Spectral Frequency Display view of the Editor panel later in this lesson and in Lesson 4, "Repairing and Adjusting Audio Clips."

3   To listen to the sound file you just opened, click the Play button (▶) in the group of transport control buttons at the bottom of the Editor panel.

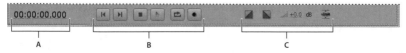

A. Timecode control. B. Transport controls. C. Quick Editing controls.

4   Either let the music play until it stops automatically at the end of the file, or stop playback earlier by clicking the Stop button (■) located to the left of the Play button.

Browsing for files

If you are not sure of the exact location or name of the file you want to open, or you would like to preview (actually, prehear) the content before opening the file in Soundbooth, you can browse for the file using Adobe Bridge.

1   Do one of the following:

• To access Bridge in Soundbooth, choose File > Browse. In Bridge, navigate to the Lesson 3 folder you copied to your hard disk.

> 💡 *If this is the first time you are using Bridge and you need help on how to locate files and folders stored on your hard disk, choose Help > Bridge Help and search for "Navigate files and folders" in the Adobe Help Viewer.*

• To open Bridge at the location of a file you have already open in Soundbooth, select that file—in this case the file GuitarRiff_from_Vinyl.wav—in the Files panel, and then choose File > Reveal in Bridge.

2   In Bridge, you will see three files in the Content panel: GuitarRiff_from_Vinyl.wav, PhatFunkyBass08-E_mono.wav, and Tiger.avi.

3   Select the first file in the Content panel, GuitarRiff_from_Vinyl.wav, and look at the Preview panel. Bridge will display a generic thumbnail image for sound files in the Preview panel and start playback of the music. In fact, it will playback the sound file repeatedly until you do one of the following:

• Choose File > Deselect, or click in and empty area in the Content panel to deselect the file.

• Move the pointer over the Preview panel, and then click the Pause button of the transport controls that appear under the thumbnail image.

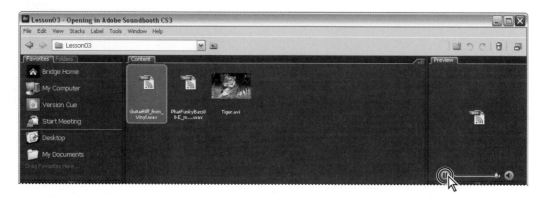

Note: Bridge will also stop playback when you switch to a different application. When switching back to Bridge, you can start playback again by clicking the Play button in the Preview panel.

For a video file like Tiger.avi in the Lesson 3 folder, Bridge will not only playback the sound but also the video portion of the file in the Preview panel.

4   When done previewing the files in the Lesson 3 folder, do one of the following:

• Click to select the file PhatFunkyBass08-E_mono.wav in the Content panel, and then choose File > Open With > Adobe Soundbooth CS3.

• Right-click (Windows) or Control-click (Mac OS) the file PhatFunkyBass08-E_ mono.wav in the Content panel, and then choose Open With > Adobe Soundbooth CS3 from the context menu.

Note: By using the menu command to open the file, you have full control over which application you want to use. On the other hand, simply double-clicking the file will open it in the default application—which might not be Soundbooth CS3—that you have assigned for that particular file type on your computer.

Back in Soundbooth, the new file is added to the list of open files in the Files panel and its waveform is displayed in the Editor panel. If you have multiple files open in Soundbooth, you can select which file to display in the Editor panel by either double-clicking its entry in the Files panel or by choosing its name from the files menu located in the top left corner of the Editor panel.

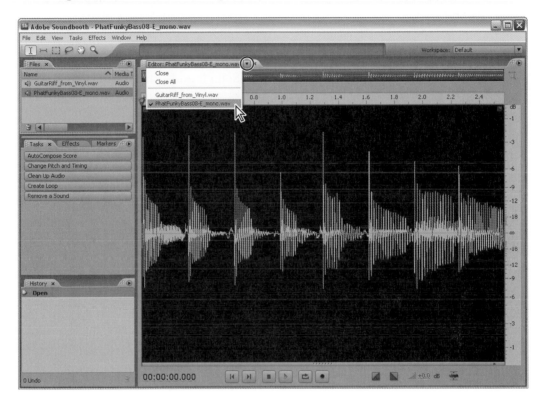

Opening files from within Adobe Premiere Pro or Adobe After Effects

Soundbooth is design to tightly integrate into your video editing workflow. If you are using Adobe Premiere Pro CS3 or Adobe After Effects CS3, you can quickly repair common audio problems in your video or audio clips using Soundbooth. Your workflow would normally look like the following:

1   In the Project panel of either Adobe Premiere Pro or Adobe After Effects, select the video or audio clip you want to edit in Soundbooth.

2   Choose Edit > Edit in Adobe Soundbooth.

3   In Soundbooth, you can perform a variety of sound editing tasks, like removing noise or unwanted background sounds, trimming the sound clip, adding fade-in and fade-out effects, adjusting volume levels, or applying special effects. See Lesson 4, "Repairing and Adjusting Audio Clips," Lesson 5, "Editing and Enhancing Voiceover Recordings," and Lesson 7, "Exploring Effects." In addition, you can use the AutoComposer to create a customized, professional soundtrack to match your video footage. You will learn all about the AutoComposer in Lesson 6, "Creating Background Music."

4   When you are done editing the file in Soundbooth, save your changes. When you return to Premiere Pro of After Effects, your changes to the audio will automatically be reflected in the project files.

Using drag and drop to open files

Last but not least, you can use the familiar drag-and-drop technique from either Windows Explorer or the Finder on Mac OS to open files in Soundbooth.

1   In Windows, do the following:

• In Windows Explorer, open My Computer by whatever method you usually use, such as double-clicking an icon on the desktop or using the Start menu.

• Navigate through the folder structure to find and open the Lesson 3 folder you copied to your hard disk.

• Drag and hold the Tiger.avi file over the Soundbooth application button in the Windows taskbar.

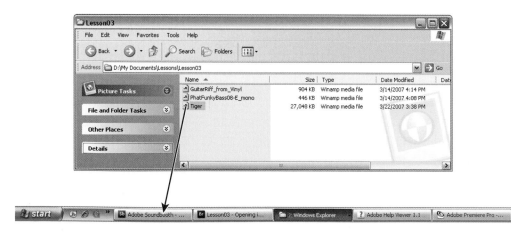

- Wait until Soundbooth becomes the foreground application, and then drag and release the pointer with the Tiger.avi icon in the Soundbooth application window.

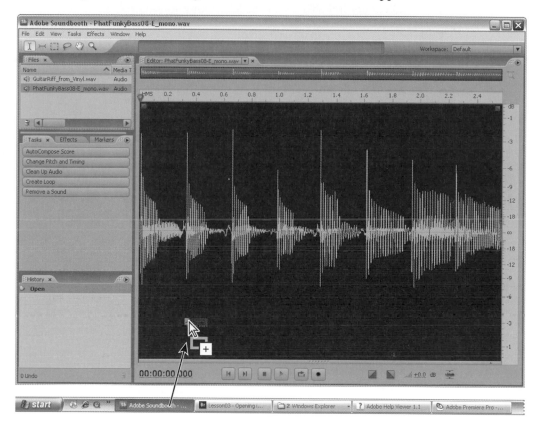

💡 *If you can arrange the Windows Explorer window and the Soundbooth application window on your screen so that you can see both windows at the same time, you can also drag and drop the file icon directly from the Windows Explorer window onto the Soundbooth application window.*

2 On Mac OS, do the following:

- In the Finder, choose File > New Finder Window.

- Navigate through the folder structure to find and open the Lesson 3 folder you copied to your hard disk.

- Drag the Tiger.avi file onto the Soundbooth application icon in the Dock. Release the pointer when the application icon becomes highlighted. *(See illustration on next page.)*

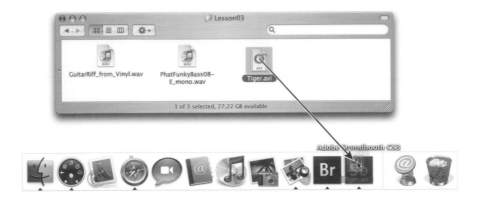

💡 *If you can arrange the Finder window and the Soundbooth application window on your screen so that you can see both windows at the same time, you can also drag and drop the file icon directly from the Finder window onto the Soundbooth application window.*

The Import Files dialog box will appear briefly while the video file is opened. Once open, the file is listed in the Files panel and its waveform is displayed in the Editor panel. In addition, the Video panel will open in a floating window and display the first frame of the movie. The Video panel will show the video portion of the file when you play its associated sound in the Editor panel.

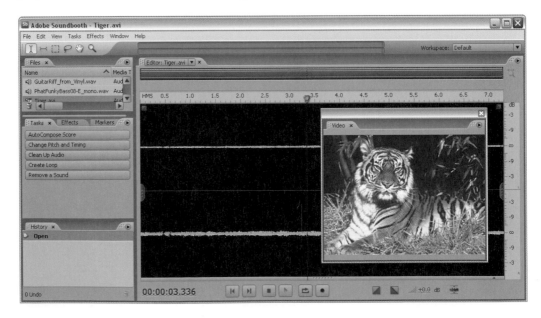

If the Video panel is obstructing your work area in the Editor panel, you can reposition it on the screen by dragging the title bar of its floating window. Or, you can choose a workspace layout that is better suited for the work with video files. You will learn more about customizing your workspace later in this lesson under "Customizing the user interface." For now, you will simply close the Video panel to get it out of the way.

3   With the Video panel open, choose Window > Video. This will close the Video panel and its floating window. The check mark in front of the menu item will disappear, indicating that this palette is now closed.

Note: The Video panel will reappear, when you switch between open files and return to a file in video format. Simply close the Video panel again if it gets in your way.

Using the Files panel

The Files panel lists all files currently open in Soundbooth and provides additional information about them, such as Media Type, Sample Rate, and Duration.

1   Use the scroll bar at the bottom of the Files panel to view the additional information available for each file.

By default, the files are sorted alphabetically by file name.

2   Click any property header to sort the files by that property. Click the same property header again to toggle between ascending and descending sort order. The current sort order is indicated by the wedge icon at the right side of the property header.

3   To change the column width for a property, position the pointer over the divider line between two property headers. When the pointer changes to the double-arrow icon (◂╟▸), click and drag the divider line to the left or right, and then release the pointer.

4   You can change the order of the properties columns by clicking the properties header and dragging it to its new location. The panel will scroll automatically, if necessary. Release the pointer when you see the black line at the insertion point.

Note: You cannot change the position of the Name properties column; it will always be the first column.

5   Select any file in the Files panel. Optionally, hold down the Ctrl key (Windows) or Command key (Mac OS) and click to select additional files. To close all files selected in the Files panel, click the Close File button (▣).

Note: The menu command File > Close will close the current file in the Editor panel, independent of the file selection made in the Files panel.

💡 *Pressing the Delete or Backspace key on your keyboard is a keyboard shortcut to close all selected files in the Files panel. For this keyboard shortcut to work, the Files panel needs to be in focus. The panel in focus has a yellow border, as shown for the Files panel in the illustration above.*

6　Reopen any file you just closed by choosing File > Open Recent > *filename*.

7　Choose Window > Files or press Ctrl+4 (Windows) or Command+4 (Mac OS) on your keyboard to close the Files panel. Choose the same command again to make the Files panel reappear.

You will learn more about customizing the user interface—including resizing, rearranging, closing or opening panels—later in this lesson under "Customizing the user interface."

8　Double-click the file name GuitarRiff_from_Vinyl.wav in the Files panel to make that file the current file in the Editor panel.

9　Choose Edit > Make Louder. Notice the asterisk (*) appended to the file name in the Files panel—as well as in the window title and the Files menu of the Editor panel—to indicate that the file has been modified.

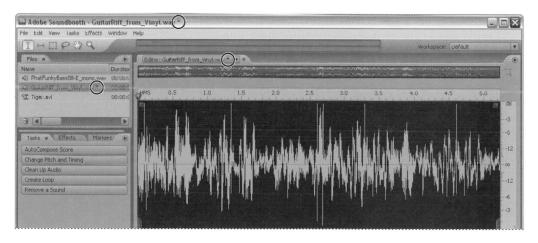

10　Choose Edit > Undo or press Ctrl+Z (Windows) or Command+Z (Mac OS) to revert the file to its original state.

Getting to know the Editor panel

Now that you know how to open files and arrange them in the Files panel, its time to explore what you can do with them in the Editor panel. Here is where you can playback the soundfiles, quickly adjust volume, add fades, or trim a track using on-clip handles, analyze and edit waveforms using the spectral frequency display, zoom in for more accurate edit tasks, make a selection, cut, copy, and paste sound snippets, and more.

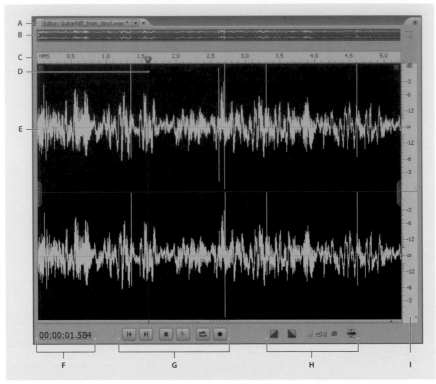

*A. Files menu. B. Zoom navigator. C. Timeline ruler. D. Current-time indicator. E. Waveform display.
F. Timecode control. G. Transport controls. H. Quick Editing controls. I. Amplitude ruler.*

1   If you can't resist, click the Play button (▶) in the group of transport control buttons at the bottom of the Editor panel to playback the sound file once—or twice. You'll get a chance to listen more to the music later in this lesson.

2   From the Files menu in the top left corner of the Editor panel, select the file PhatFunkyBass08-E_mono.wav to make it the current file.

This particular sound file was recorded in mono. Thus, only one waveform is displayed in the waveform display.

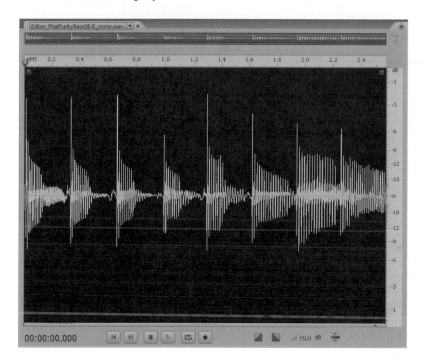

The horizontal timeline ruler across the top of the waveform display measures time, the vertical amplitude ruler measures the loudness of the sound ranging from −∞ (negative infinity) for silence to 0 dB (zero decibel) for loud peaks and troughs. You can clearly see each strike of the guitar chords in time.

Adjusting the rulers

You can choose to display a second timeline ruler at the bottom of the waveform display.

1   Select the View > Bottom Timeline Ruler menu item to add a second timeline ruler at the bottom of the display. Deselect View > Bottom Timeline Ruler to have only one timeline ruler at the top.

Note: You can't hide the top timeline ruler.

The vertical ruler can be placed at either the left or the right side, or at both sides.

2   Toggle the visibility of a vertical ruler on either side of the waveform display by choosing View > Vertical Ruler > Left or View > Vertical Ruler > Right.

Note: You can have one or two vertical rulers, but not none.

The timeline ruler supports many different units of time to suit your editing needs.

3   Right-click (Windows) or Control-click (Mac OS) the timeline ruler at the top, and then select from the context menu one of the following options:

• HMS, to show hours, minutes, and seconds (and decimals of a second) with no leading zeros (e.g. 3:45.5 for three minutes, 45 and a half seconds).

• Decimal, to show hours, minutes, seconds, and milliseconds including leading and trailing zeros in the form hh:mm:ss:mmm (e.g. 00:03:45.500 for zero hours, three minutes, 45 seconds, and 500 milliseconds).

• Samples, to show only the samples (e.g. 44100 would be one second into the song at a sample rate of 44100 samples per second).

• Any of the FPS (frames per second) options, to show the time and frame number in the format hh:mm:ss:frames. There are predefined fps options for various standard film and video formats, and one custom option (see Edit Custom Time Format below). These options are useful when working on audio files intended for use in a video or Flash project.

• Edit Custom Time Format, to open the General panel of the Preferences dialog box. Here you can enter a custom frames per second value if needed, and choose to show only frames, or time and frame in the format hh:mm:ss:frames. The default value of 12 fps matches the default fps value used in Adobe Flash Professional.

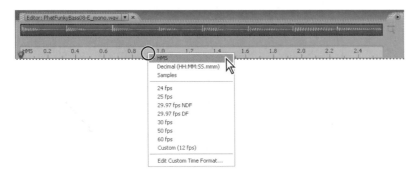

💡 *If you are working with two timeline rulers, you can select different units of time for the top and the bottom timeline ruler.*

Selecting channel view options

If you are working with mono files, there's only one waveform to deal with. Stereo files contain two waveforms, one for the left channel and one for the right channel.

1   From the Files menu in the top left corner of the Editor panel, select the file GuitarRiff_from_Vinyl.wav to make it the current file.

You will see two waveforms, with the waveform of the left channel above the waveform of the right channel. Each channel has its own vertical amplitude ruler.

Should you ever come across a sound file recorded in 5.1 surround-sound format, you would see six channels as shown in the illustration below (there is no waveform visible in the last channel because it is silent here). From top to bottom you see the waveforms for the Left, Right, Left Surround, Right Surround, Center, and LFE (low-frequency effects) channel.

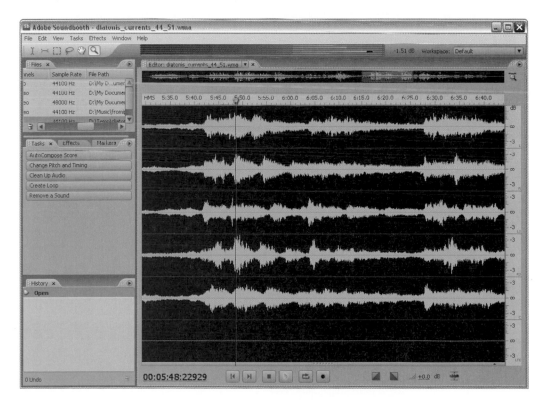

Displaying each channel separately can be helpful to reveal distinct volume changes per channel, like the strikes in the guitar sound sample. If you are more interested to see the overall volume change in your sound clip, you can display all channels layered one on top of the other.

2   Choose View > Channels > Layered to see both waveforms of the GuitarRiff_from_ Vinyl.wav sound file combined, with the right channel in blue overlapping the left channel in green.

In the case of the GuitarRiff_from_Vinyl.wav sound file, the two waveforms are almost identical. The illustration below, a section taken from David Bowie's *Changes*, is better suited to illustrate the usefulness of viewing channels separated versus layered.

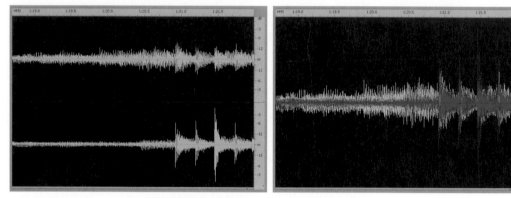

Two channels of a sound file viewed separated (left) and layered (right).

3   Choose View > Channels > Separated to return to the separated channel view.

Revealing the spectral frequency display

In addition to being able to display waveforms, whether one, two, or more channels, separated or layered, Soundbooth can also display the content of a sound file sorted by its frequency components (ranging from low bass to high treble). This unique way of displaying sound enables you to easily recognize unwanted sound artifacts and to quickly remove them using Marquee and Lasso tools similar to those found in Adobe Photoshop software. This is also known as *frequency-space editing*.

To give you an idea of how this works, let's look at the spectral frequency display of our three sound files.

1   If not already selected, choose the file GuitarRiff_from_Vinyl.wav from the Files menu of the Editor panel.

2   Choose View > Spectral Frequency Display or press Shift+F on your keyboard.

The Editor panel now displays the waveform in a tiny band at the top, and the spectral frequency display takes up most of the view.

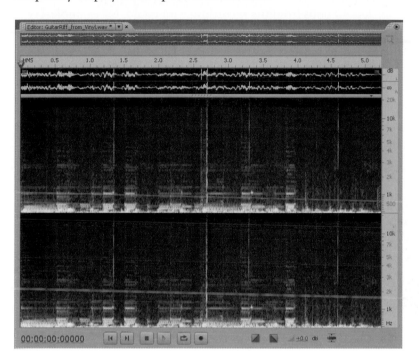

The vertical rulers for the frequency display measure frequency, starting with low frequencies at the bottom and going to high frequencies at the top. If the sound has a component of a specific frequency, then there is color in the frequency display at that frequency. The difference in color represents amplitude, ranging from dark blue for low amplitude to bright yellow for high amplitude. Black means silence at that particular frequency.

For the GuitarRiff_from_Vinyl.wav file you see higher amplitudes (brighter yellows) in the lower frequencies. But you also see a lot of color, even if at lower amplitudes, practically throughout the entire frequency spectrum. This is characteristic for noise.

Bright vertical bars that extend from top to bottom (you can see examples in the above illustration near the 1.3 second mark, the 2.7 second mark, the 3.3 second mark, and the 4.6 second mark) are characteristic for clicks and pops.

3   Click the Play button and pay attention to the clicks and pops in the recording. Notice how they coincide with the current-time indicator passing over these bright vertical bars in the spectral frequency display.

To remove the clicks and pops from the recording, you could, for example, try to select these bars in the spectral display, and then lower their volume. But don't do that now. Soundbooth has automated many of these standard editing tasks for you, as you will learn in Lesson 4, "Repairing and Adjusting Audio Clips."

4   From the Files menu in the top left corner of the Editor panel, select the file PhatFunkyBass08-E_mono.wav to make it the current file.

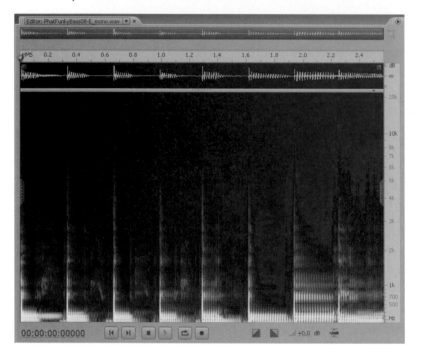

What a difference! There is no noise or any clicks or pops visible in the spectral display, and if you play the sound you'll hear none of these. A very clean recording.

Note: There is only one channel displayed, because this is a mono recording.

5   Select the file Tiger.avi from the Files menu in the Editor panel. Close the Video panel if it pops up and gets in your way.

Quite obviously, this sound file has some major deficiencies. There are gaps in the recording near the 0.5 second mark and the 6 second mark. The black vertical bars indicate complete silence for a couple of milliseconds. At around the same points in time, you can see a pattern of several square dots at about 3.5 kHz, 6 kHz, and 14 kHz, more pronounced in the right channel displayed at the top than in the left channel at the bottom. If you listen to the file, you can recognize these as ringing sounds. In fact, a recording of a phone ringing in the background would look very similar to these patterns. Such individual, unwanted sounds in a recording can easily be selected in the spectral view using the marquee or lasso tool, and then removed.

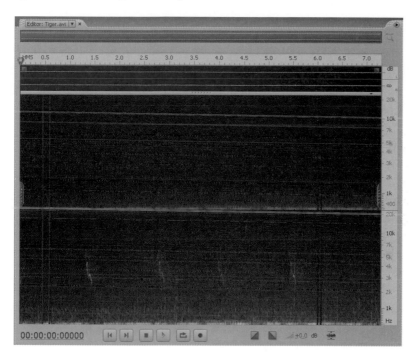

Adjusting the spectral frequency display

You can adjust the height of the spectral frequency display, leaving more or less room for the waveform display.

1   To adjust the height of the spectral frequency display, position the pointer over the divider line between the waveform and the spectral frequency display. When the pointer changes to the double horizontal bar with arrows icon, click and drag the divider line up or down. Then, release the pointer.

2   Move the divider line all the way down to show only the waveform display, move the divider line all the way up to show only the frequency spectrum display.

3   Move the divider line back towards the center of the display.

4   Choose View > Spectral Frequency Display to close the spectral frequency display. Choose View > Spectral Frequency Display again—or press Shift+F on your keyboard—to reopen the spectral frequency display. Notice how Soundbooth remembers the position of the divider bar where you last positioned it in step 3.

5   Double-clicking the divider bar or clicking the little black triangle located at the right end of the divider bar is equivalent to choosing View > Spectral Frequency Display from the menu, or pressing Shift+F on your keyboard. Try it!

If you have a mouse with a scroll wheel, you can use the scroll wheel to adjust the scale used for the frequency ruler from linear to logarithmic. Alternatively (or if you don't have a mouse with a scroll wheel), you can change the Vertical Scale value in the Remove a Sound section of the Tasks panel.

6   If you have a mouse with a scroll wheel, place the pointer over the spectral frequency display of the Editor panel, and then roll the mouse wheel. Roll up to expand the lower frequencies and compress the higher frequencies in the display. Roll all the way down for a linear scale.

7   Place your pointer over the blue number for the Vertical Scale in the Remove a Sound section of the Tasks panel. Click and drag to the right for a logarithmic scale (Vertical Scale value of up to 95%), or click and drag all the way to the left (Vertical Scale value of 0%) for a linear scale.

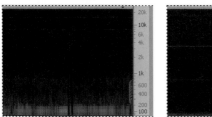

The scale of the frequency ruler can be adjusted by using the mouse wheel, or by changing the Vertical Scale value in the Remove a Sound section of the Tasks panel.

💡 *With your pointer positioned over the waveform display of the Editor panel, you can use the mouse wheel to zoom into a specific time range or zoom out again.*

The Editor panel when using the AutoComposer

There is one more view of the Editor panel that looks distinctively different from the waveform and spectral frequency display views you've seen so far: The Editor view when working with the AutoComposer and Soundbooth scores.

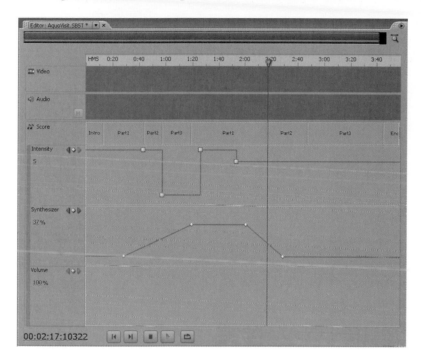

You will learn all about working with the AutoComposer and Soundbooth scores in Lesson 6, "Creating Background Music."

Positioning the current-time indicator

1   Select the file GuitarRiff_from_Vinyl.wav from the Files menu in the Editor panel.

2   If necessary, click the Go To Previous Marker button (▶), located in the group of transport controls at the bottom of the Editor panel, until the Timecode control reads zero.

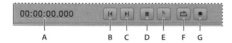

A. Timecode control.
B. Go To Previous Marker. C. Go To Next Marker. D. Stop. E. Play. F. Loop Playback. G. Record.

3 Click the Play button (▶). As you listen to the music, notice the current-time indicator (♥) moving across the waveform, while the timecode control is displaying the current time in numerical format.

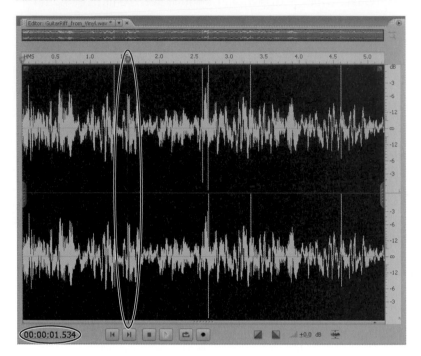

💡 *Right-click (Windows) or Control-click (Mac OS) the timecode control in the lower left corner of the Editor panel, and then choose any of the available display formats from the context menu. You can choose independently which units of time to use for the timecode control, the top timeline ruler, and the bottom timeline ruler.*

4 Click anywhere in the timeline ruler to position the current-time indicator at that point in time. Click the Play button (▶) to start playback. Playback always starts at the position of the current-time indicator.

💡 *When the Editor panel is in focus, as indicated by a yellow border around the panel, you can press the spacebar to start and stop playback. When playback is stopped, press the Home key to jump to beginning of the file, or press the End key to jump to the end. Use the left and right arrow keys to reposition the current-time indicator in small increments. Hold down the Alt key (Windows) or Option key (Mac OS) while pressing the arrow keys to jump five steps at a time.*

5   Click and drag the current-time indicator in the timeline ruler to *scrub* the audio, previewing it at different time points.

6   Position the pointer over the timecode control. When the cursor changes to the hand with double-arrow icon, click and drag to the left or right to reposition the current-time indicator.

7   Click the timecode control, and then enter a time code in the text field that appears. Press the enter or return keys to confirm your entry and position the current-time indicator at the specified location.

8   Use the J, K, and L keys on the keyboard to mimic a shuttle control. Press the L key once to start forward playback, press the L key again to double the speed, and again to arrive at four times playback speed. Press the K key to stop playback. Press the J key once, twice, or three times to play backwards at normal, double, or four times normal speed, respectively. The higher playback speed becomes useful only when scanning for edit points in longer source files than the sample clips provided here.

Playing selections

1   In the Tools panel, select the Time Selection tool ( ).

Tools panel controls:
A. Time Selection tool. **B.** *Frequency Selection tool.* **C.** *Rectangular Marquee tool.* **D.** *Lasso tool.*
E. *Hand tool.* **F.** *Zoom tool.* **G.** *Level meters.* **H.** *Workspace menu.*

2   In the waveform display, click and drag to select about one second of music, and then release the pointer.

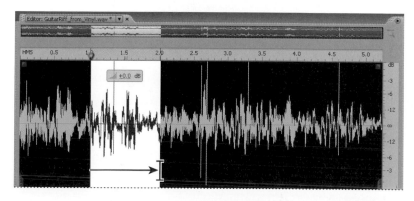

3 Press the spacebar or click the Play button (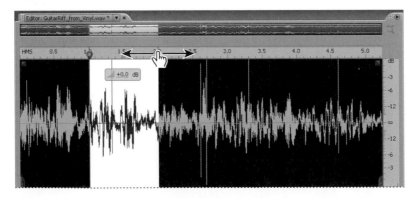) to start playback. Notice that playback starts at the beginning of the selection. However, it does not stop at the end of the selection but continues to play until it reaches the end of the file.

4 In the group of transport controls at the bottom of the Editor panel, click the Loop Playback button ( ) to activate it. The arrow in the button's icon turns green when Loop Playback is activated ( ).

5 Start playback and notice that playback starts at the beginning of the selection, plays to the end of the selection, and then immediately starts again at the beginning of the selection. Playback continues to loop the selection until you explicitly stop playback. Click the Stop button or press the spacebar to stop playback.

Note: If there is no selection, loop playback will loop over the entire length of the sound clip.

6 (Optional) Click the Go To Previous Marker button and the Go To Next Marker button. Notice that the beginning and end of a selection—as well as the beginning and end or the in and out points of the entire clip—are treated like *markers*. You will learn how to use and define additional markers in Lesson 8, "Working with Markers."

7 To change the length of the selection, position the pointer over either the beginning or end of the selection in the timeline. When the pointer changes to the pointer hand icon ( ), click and drag to either side to adjust the selection length, and then release the pointer.

8 To reposition the selection within the sound clip, position the pointer over the handle at the center of the selection in the timeline. When the pointer changes to the hand icon (✋), click and drag to either side to reposition the selection, and then release the pointer.

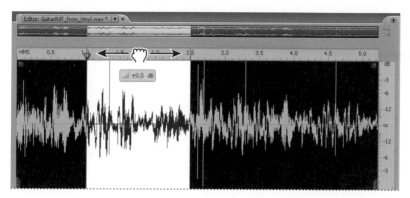

Note: *Selections are used in many ways. In general, edit tasks are restricted to the current selection: you can increase or lower the volume of a selection, perform the usual cut, copy and paste operations on the selection, or apply effects to just the selected area of the music. You can also export a selection as a separate file in various formats, create a loop from the selection, or zoom in to have the selection fill the width of the Editor panel display.*

Zooming in and out

If you are working with longer clips, you will normally not want to display the entire waveform in the Editor panel display, but zoom in at a specific point in time to increase the level of detail you can see.

1   To zoom in on the Editor panel display, do one of the following:

•   With a selection active, choose View > Zoom In at the In Point, View > Zoom In at the Out Point, or View > Zoom To Selection, to zoom to the respective areas of the selection. The keyboard shortcuts are Shift+Q, Shift+W, and Shift+A, respectively. With no active selection, these commands will zoom to the in or out points of the file, or the location of the current-time indicator.

•   Click the Zoom Out Full button (⊡) located in the top right corner of the Editor panel, or choose View > Zoom Out Full, to display the entire audio file again. The keyboard shortcut is the backslash key (\).

- Choose View > Zoom In, or View > Zoom Out, to zoom in or out at the location of the current-time indicator. Or, use the equal sign key (=) or minus sign key (-) as keyboard shortcuts.

- Position the pointer over the Editor panel, and then use the mouse wheel to zoom in or out.

Note: If the pointer is positioned over the Spectral Frequency display, using the mouse wheel will adjust the scale used in the frequency ruler, not the zoom level in the waveform display.

- In the Tools panel, select the Zoom tool (🔍). Click in the waveform display to zoom in. Hold down the Alt key (Windows) or Option key (Mac OS) to zoom out. Or, click and drag in the waveform display to zoom in on a specific range of the waveform.

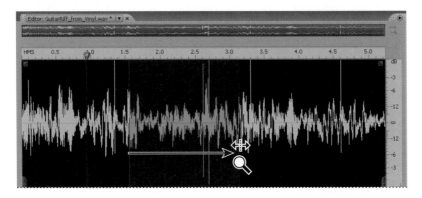

- To quickly zoom in on a specific range of the waveform without having to select the Zoom tool first, right-click (Windows) or Control-click (Mac OS) the timeline ruler or the zoom navigator, and then drag the pointer to make your selection.

Without having to select the Zoom tool first, right-click (Windows) or Control-click (Mac OS) the timeline ruler or the zoom navigator, and then drag the pointer to select the area you want to zoom in on.

2   When the view is not fully zoomed out, you can use the zoom navigator, located at the top of the Editor panel, to navigate to a different position in the file. Position the pointer over the highlighted section in the zoom navigator. When the pointer changes to the hand icon (✋), click and drag to a new position in the file, and then release the pointer.

💡 *Alternatively to using the zoom navigator, you can select the Hand tool in the Tools panel, and then click and drag the waveform display—or the spectral frequency display—to navigate to a different location in the file.*

This concludes the first part of this lesson, "Exploring the User Interface." You should now feel comfortable using the Files panel, and navigating in the Editor panel. There is still more to learn about the Editor panel, as well as the other panels not covered in this lesson. You will learn all about the Tasks panel in Lesson 4, "Repairing and Adjusting Audio Clips," Lesson 5, "Editing and Enhancing Voiceover Recordings," and Lesson 6, "Creating Background Music." The Effects panel is discussed in Lesson 7, "Exploring Effects," and the Markers panel in Lesson 8, "Working with Markers." Other panels, like the History panel and Video panel, will be introduced along the way where appropriate. The remainder of this lesson will teach you how to use predefined workspaces and how to adjust them to suit your needs.

Customizing the user interface

Soundbooth is designed to cover a wide range of post-production sound tasks. These range from simple audio editing and clean-up tasks to sound design and music creation for video and animation projects. To enable you to work most productively, the user interface should be adaptable to the task at hand. For example, when creating background music for a video project you would want to see the video playing while working in the sound editor panel. In other situations, having a video panel visible might not be necessary and you would not want it to take away precious screen real estate. The solution Soundbooth provides is predefined workspaces that optimize the layout of panels for specific tasks.

Selecting predefined workspaces

When you first launch Soundbooth, it will open using its default workspace. You were using this workspace all along in the beginning of this lesson. In addition to the "Default" workspace, Soundbooth ships with two more predefined workspaces, namely "Edit Audio to Video," a panel layout best suited to precisely synchronizing audio and video, and "Edit Score to Video," to facilitate creating background music with scores using the AutoComposer.

1 Select the file Tiger.avi from the Files menu in the Editor panel.

With the default workspace selected, the Video panel will open in a floating window. To work with video, the Edit Audio to Video workspace might be the better choice.

2 Choose Window > Workspace > Edit Audio to Video, or select Edit Audio to Video from the workspace menu located in the top right corner of the Editor panel.

The Video panel gets docked next to the Markers panel above the Editor panel that now has a reduced height to make room for the additional panels.

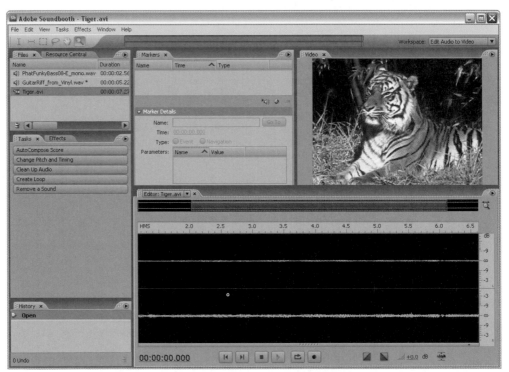

The Soundbooth user interface with the Edit Audio to Video workspace selected.

The panel layout in the Edit Score to Video workspace is only slightly different. But even little changes in the layout can dramatically increase your efficiency. Depending on your work style, you may find that you would prefer to have one panel positioned here, and another panel over there. The size of your screen and whether you are working with one or two monitors also plays a role in how to best arrange the various panels. Luckily, Soundbooth offers numerous options to help you customize your workspace.

Resizing panel groups

The application window uses frames to subdivide and organize the workspace. Each frame can contain either a single panel or a group of panels. The height and width of the frames in relation to each other is adjustable.

1   Position the pointer over the divider line to the left of the Video panel. When the cursor changes to the double-arrow icon (⬌), click and drag the divider line to the left, increasing the width of the Video panel and at the same time reducing the width of the group of panels next to it. Then, release the pointer.

2   Position the pointer over the divider line below the Video panel. Drag the divider line to the bottom, increasing the height of the Video panel and at the same time reducing the height of the Editor panel. Then, release the pointer.

3   To resize height and width of a frame at the same time, position the pointer at the intersection of the horizontal and vertical divider line. When the pointer changes to the four-way arrow icon (✛), click and drag to resize the frame. Then, release the pointer.

Closing and opening panels

To make more space for the other panels, you can close panels you are currently not using. If you close the last panel in a panel group you will automatically close its frame, making more space available for the surrounding frames. When needed, you can reopen the panels or restore the default layout of all panels in the workspace.

1   To close the Video panel, do one of the following:

- Choose Window > Video.

- Click the Close button (✖) on the Video panel.

- Choose Close Panel from the panel menu.

> 💡 *If the frame contains more than one panel, you can close all panels in that group at the same time by choosing Close Frame from the panel menu.*

2   To reopen the Video panel, choose Window > Video.

3   At any time you can return to the default layout of panels for the current workspace by choosing Window > Workspace > Reset "*workspace name*" or Reset "*workspace name*" from the Workspace menu in the Editor panel, and then clicking OK in the Reset Workspace dialog box.

Opening panels in floating windows

At times it can be useful to have a panel or a group of panels placed in a floating window. You can, for example, position a floating window on a second monitor and gain space for the other panels on the main monitor.

1   To open a panel in a floating window, do one of the following:

• Choose Undock Panel from the panel menu.

• Press the Ctrl key (Windows) or Command key (Mac OS), and then click the panel gripper and drag the panel away from its current position.

When you see the ghosted floating window, release the pointer, and then release the Ctrl key (Windows) or Command key (Mac OS).

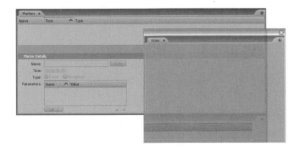

• Click the panel gripper and drag the panel outside the application window. If the application window is occupying the entire screen, drag the panel to the taskbar (Windows) or menu bar (Mac OS).

2   To open a panel group in a floating window, do one of the following:

• Choose Undock Frame from the panel menu.

• Press the Ctrl key (Windows) or Command key (Mac OS), and then click the group gripper and drag the panel group away from its current position.

When you see the ghosted floating window, release the pointer, and then release the Ctrl key (Windows) or Command key (Mac OS).

• Click the group gripper and drag the panel group outside the application window. If the application window is occupying the entire screen, drag the panel group to the taskbar (Windows) or menu bar (Mac OS).

Docking panels

The opposite of closing a frame, or opening it in a floating window to allow the adjacent frame to expand, is to dock a panel or frame next to an existing frame, causing it to become smaller to make space for the new frame.

1 To dock a panel next to an existing frame, click the panel gripper and drag the panel over an existing frame. Do not release the pointer yet. Notice the different drop zones as they get highlighted when you hover over them with the pointer. Release the pointer when the desired docking zone is highlighted; dropping the frame on the left or right docking zone will position the frames next to each other, dropping it on the top or bottom zone will position them above each other.

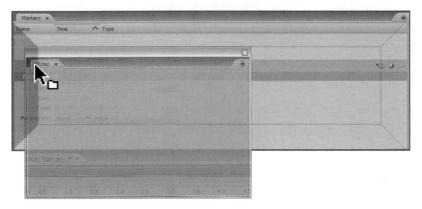

2 To dock a panel group next to an existing frame, click the group gripper and drag the panel group over an existing frame. Release the pointer when the desired docking zone is highlighted.

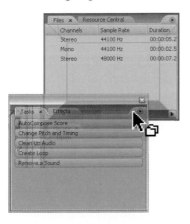

Grouping panels

You can easily change which panels are grouped with each other. Simply drag a panel out of one group and drag it into another group.

1 To group a panel with an existing panel group, click the panel gripper and drag the panel over an existing frame. Release the pointer when either of the two grouping zones is highlighted: the drop zone along the tab area or the drop zone in the middle of a panel or panel group.

💡 *Drag the group gripper to add an entire panel group to an existing panel or panel group. This will also close the empty frame of the group that was moved.*

2 To change the order of the panels within a group, click the panel gripper and drag the panel to the new position. Then, release the pointer.

Saving customized workspaces

Soundbooth remembers your current layout of panels—your customized workspace—until you choose to reset it to its default settings. If you have created a workspace that works well for your requirements, you might want to save the settings under a new name so that you can reset to this particular workspace at any time. You can create and save multiple workspaces for different tasks.

1   Customize your workspace by resizing frames, opening, closing, docking or grouping panels, as you've just learned in this lesson.

2   Choose Window > Workspace > New Workspace or choose New Workspace from the Workspace menu in the Editor panel.

3   In the New Workspace dialog box, enter a name that best describes your customized workspace, and then click OK.

The new name is now added to the Workspace menu and you can reset to its saved settings should you make further changes to your workspace.

4   To delete a workspace name from the workspace menu, first switch to a workspace other than the one you want to delete. Then choose Window > Workspace > Delete Workspace, or choose Delete Workspace from the Workspace menu in the Editor panel.

5   In the Delete Workspace dialog box, select the name from the name menu, and then click OK.

Note: The name will disappear from the workspace list and its saved settings are lost.

Review

▶ **Review questions**

1   Name four methods of opening files in Soundbooth.

2   What is the current-time indicator?

3   What is the difference between the waveform display and the spectral frequency display?

4   What is a workspace?

5   What are docking and grouping zones?

▶ **Review answers**

1   Invoke the Open Files dialog box; Browse for files in Bridge, and then choose File > Open With > Adobe Soundbooth CS3; Drag and drop files from Windows Explorer (Windows) or Finder (Mac OS) onto the Soundbooth application window; Select a sound or video file in Adobe Premiere Pro or Adobe After Effects, and then choose Edit > Edit in Adobe Soundbooth.

2   The current-time indicator in the Editor panel determines the starting position for playback and moves through the waveform as you listen to audio files.

3   The waveform display shows audio as a series of amplitude peaks and troughs while the spectral frequency display shows audio by its frequency components. The former is perfect to identify amplitude changes like drum beats or beginnings and endings of spoken words, while the latter is better suited to analyze which frequencies are most prevalent in the sound file, or to remove specific sounds like a cell phone ring from the recording.

4   A workspace is the current layout of panels and panel groups in the Soundbooth user interface. There are predefined workspaces for typical sound editing tasks. You can also customize your workspace and save the settings to suit your particular needs.

5 When rearranging panels or panel groups in your workspace, docking and grouping zones determine how the panels are placed relative to a frame when the pointer is released. When released over one of the four docking zones, the panels are placed next to the existing frame. When released over one of the two dropping zones, the panels are grouped with the other panel or panels in the frame.

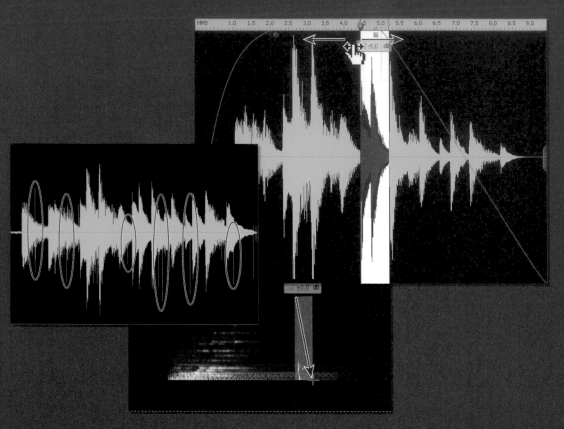

Adobe Soundbooth CS3 helps you match the clarity of your audio with that of your visuals, providing focused tools to clean up unwanted noise like hissing, clicks, and pops from your audio tracks, or to polish voiceovers in a single stroke.

4 | Repairing and Adjusting Audio Clips

Adobe Soundbooth lets you edit, optimize, and repair audio using intuitive visual tools. With a few clicks you can rescue old or low quality sound recordings that seemed beyond repair.

Specialized tools help you to eliminate clicks and pops from a recording, or to remove unwanted background sounds. With on-clip controls, you can trim, fade, and adjust volume directly in the waveform display.

In this lesson, you will do the following:

- Remove clicks and pops from a recording.
- Set noise prints and remove noise.
- Remove unwanted sounds.
- Trim clips, delete or silence sections.
- Create a fade in and a fade out.
- Adjust volume.

Before you begin, make sure that you have correctly copied the Lessons folder from the CD in the back of this book onto your computer's hard disk. See "Copying the Classroom in a Book files" on page 2.

Getting started

In this lesson, you'll be utilizing Adobe Soundbooth's built-in noise reduction and sound removal tools to improve the sound quality of a not-so-perfect recording from a vinyl record. Next, you'll identify unwanted background sounds in the spectral frequency display—

and remove them. Finally, you'll perform some common sound-editing tasks using the quick-editing and on-clip controls in the Editor panel.

Before you begin, perform the following steps to ensure that you start the lesson with the default window layout.

1 Start Adobe Soundbooth.

2 Select Window > Workspace > Default, if it is not already selected. Then, choose Window > Workspace > Reset "Default."

3 In the Reset Workspace dialog box, click OK.

Noise reduction

Because many recordings do not take place in a professional recording studio, noise is typically recorded along with the focus of your recording. Noise can be described as undesirable or unwanted signals—usually at lower amplitudes—that are picked up by the microphone during the recording session. Street noise, a cell phone ringing in the background, or the buzz of a nearby electronic device—such as a fan, are all examples of noise that can get recorded unintentionally.

Noise and imperfections in a recording may also be related to the recording source itself. Creating a digital recording from an analog source, such as a record player, may result in clicks and pops throughout the recording, due to dust, scratches or other flaws in the vinyl record.

In the first part of this lesson, you'll be repairing a waveform containing noise that is typical for recordings taken from old vinyl records.

1 Choose File > Open.

2 In the Open Files dialog box that appears, navigate to your Lesson04 folder you copied to your hard disk. Within that folder, select the file Solace_04_Start.wav, and then click Open.

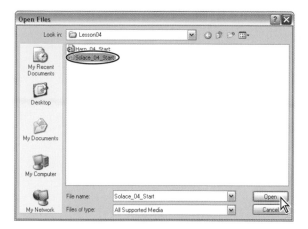

3 Press the spacebar to begin playback. While listening, notice the imperfections in the recording. Background noise and several clicks and pops are apparent throughout the piece. In the waveform display, you can visually identify noise at the very beginning of the file where no instrument is playing, and spikes produced by clicks and pops at several places in the waveform.

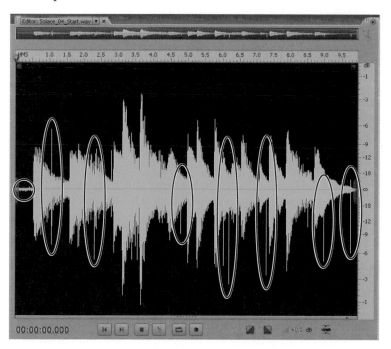

Removing clicks and pops

The Clean Up Audio task contains a specialized tool for removing sharp clicks and pops (such as crackle from vinyl records), which is exactly what we want to do.

1 Choose Tasks > Clean Up Audio, or select the Tasks panel, and then click Clean Up Audio, to reveal the Clean Up Audio section in the Tasks panel.

2 Click the Clicks & Pops button to open the Clicks & Pops dialog box.

3 Click the Preview button in the Clicks & Pops dialog box, and then drag the Click/Pop slider slowly to the right until you no longer notice any clicks and pops. We used a value of approximately 33%.

With the Click/Pop slider in the Clicks & Pops dialog box, you can determine the tool's sensitivity to audio artifacts. Higher settings will remove more artifacts, but as the correction becomes more aggressive, audio you wish to retain might be removed. Use lower values to remove subtle clicks, or higher values to remove loud pops. If necessary, you can select part of the waveform in the waveform display before opening the Clicks & Pops dialog box, thereby restricting the correction to only the selected portion.

4 To compare processed and original audio, click the Power button (⏻).

5 When you have found the setting with the best-sounding result, click Stop to turn off preview, and then click OK to close the Clicks & Pops dialog box and to apply the adjustment to the original file.

Creating a noise print

Removing background noise from a recording is almost as easy as removing clicks and pops. But before clicking the Noise button in the Clean Up Audio section of the Tasks panel, you should create a noise print as reference. Creating a noise print is optional, but can help Soundbooth to do a better job when removing noise.

To create a good noise print, try to find a section in the recording that contains only noise, like the first half-second in the file Solace_04_Start.wav.

1 In the Tools panel, select the Time Selection tool (⌶).

2 In the waveform display, click and drag to select some of the noise in the first half-second of the waveform, and then release the pointer.

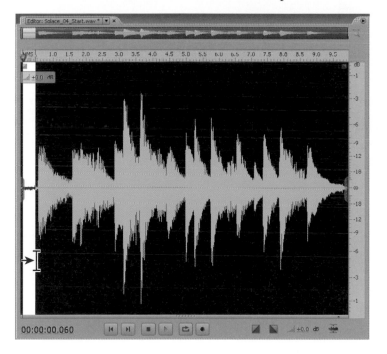

3 In the Tasks panel, click the Capture Noise Print button to capture a noise print based on the current selection in the waveform display.

Removing noise

You will now be using the noise print you've just created to cancel out the noise present throughout the file.

1   Using the Time Selection tool, click—don't drag—anywhere in the waveform to clear the current selection.

💡 *You can restrict the noise reduction to a portion of the sound file, by selecting that area before invoking the noise reduction task.*

2   Under Clean Up Audio in the Tasks panel, click the Noise button.

The Noise dialog box will open, offering two sliders to control how the noise reduction works. The Reduction slider determines how aggressive Soundbooth is at determining what is and what isn't noise. Use lower values for audio with a wide dynamic range, such as classical music with loud and quiet passages. Use higher values for audio with a compressed dynamic range, such as pop music. With the Reduce By slider you can adjust how much to attenuate the portions considered as noise.

3   If not already selected, click to select the Use Captured Noise Print check box.

4   Click the Preview button in the Noise dialog box, and then adjust the Reduction and Reduce By sliders. Start out with a relatively aggressive Reduction setting, and then drag the Reduce By slider to the right until you hear the noise drop out. Continue to move both sliders back and forth until you get optimal results. We used the values 70.6% for Reduction and 14 dB for Reduce By.

5   To compare processed and original audio, click the Power button (⏻).

6   When you have found the settings with the best-sounding result, click Stop to turn off preview, and then click OK to apply the adjustment to the file, and close the Noise dialog box.

7   Choose File > Save As. In the Save As dialog box, keeping the Windows Waveform file type selected, change the file name to **Solace_04_End.wav**, and then click Save to save the file in the Lesson04 folder on your hard disk. Click OK in the Save As Options dialog box without making any changes to the settings.

8   (Optional) Close the file Solace_04_Start.wav without saving any changes.

Recording tips

While many tools can make a recording sound better after it's finished, nothing can substitute for making it sound good to begin with. Here are a few ways to make the best possible recording—even without a recording studio:

• Record in a quiet environment whenever possible. Soundbooth can take out noise later, but it's best if the room is quiet to begin with.

• Buy yourself a better microphone. The one that came with your computer will rarely capture good-quality audio. You can find good microphones for less than $100, and starting with a good microphone gives you much more flexibility later.

• Find a room with carpet, and perhaps upholstered furniture and drapes. A room with too many hard surfaces will cause echoes.

• If you don't like how a recording sounds, move around the room. Change the way you're facing or where you're sitting. Try putting a pillow in the corner and talking toward it. You can get a great sound without a professional studio, but you'll need to experiment to figure out where your room sounds best.

• Record with one second of silence at the beginning or end that can be used as a noise print.

—Hart Shafer, product manager for Adobe audio products

Sound removal

In some cases, Soundbooth needs your help in identifying which sounds to remove and which to keep. There is simply no telling whether the cell phone ring in the background is intentional or not, or whether you want to keep the cough sound in the middle of the recording or remove it. Your sound editing needs might even change from one day to the next, depending on your task at hand.

The spectral frequency display can help you to quickly identify a specific sound in your recording. To remove that sound is only a matter of selecting it, and then clicking a button or moving a slider.

Removing unwanted sound in the spectral frequency display

In this part of the lesson, you'll be removing a cough sound from the recording of a harp playing.

1   Choose File > Open.

2   In the Open Files dialog box that appears, navigate to your Lesson04 folder you copied to your hard disk. Within that folder, select the file Harp_04_Start.wav, and then click Open.

3   Press the spacebar to begin playback. While listening, notice the cough sound towards the end of the recording. In the waveform display, the cough is visible as a sudden spike in the waveform (in both channels of the stereo file).

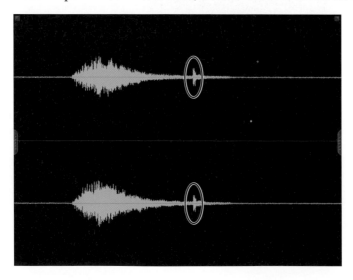

4   Choose Tasks > Remove a Sound, or select the Tasks panel, and then click Remove a Sound, to reveal the Remove a Sound section in the Tasks panel.

The spectral frequency display opens. The cough is visible as a sudden spike in the higher frequencies (in both channels) towards the end of the harp recording.

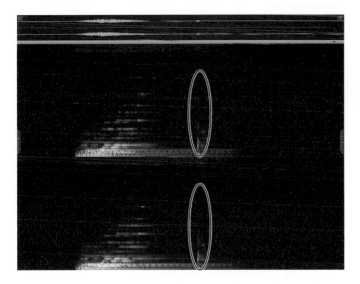

5   Select the Marquee tool (⬚) in either the Tools panel or the Remove a Sound section in the Tasks panel. Or, use the keyboard shortcut M.

6   Click and drag a marquee selection around the spectral representation of the cough. Do not include the lower frequencies—containing most of the harp sound—in the selection, as shown in the illustration below.

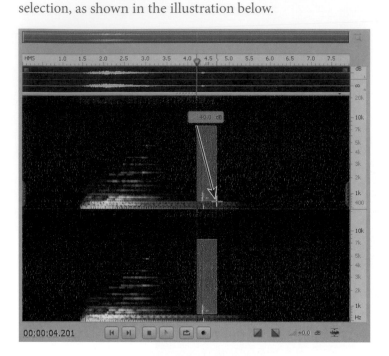

7   To silence the cough sound, do one of the following:

• With the Editor panel in focus, choose Edit > Delete, or press the Delete key.

• Position the cursor over the blue number in the volume pop-up bubble above the selected audio, or next to the volume icon (◢) at the bottom of the Editor panel. When the pointer changes to the hand with two arrows icon (✋), click and drag to the left until the blue number reads -96 dB. Then, release the pointer.

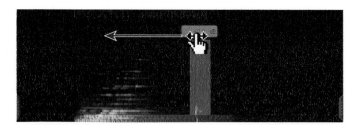

• Click the blue number and enter a value of **-96**, and then press Enter.

Note: *96 dB is the dynamic range of a recording sampled with a bit depth of 16, as is the case for the file Harp_04_Start.wav. Therefore, reducing the volume by -96 dB completely silences the selected audio. For more information about the relation between bit depth and dynamic range, search for "bit depth" in Soundbooth Help.*

The Applying effect dialog box is displayed briefly, and then all sound in the selected area is deleted.

8 Click once anywhere in the spectral frequency display to clear the current selection. Notice the black area, from which all sound has been removed.

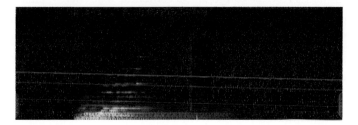

9 Position the current-time indicator at the beginning of the file and press the spacebar to begin playback.

The cough sound has been almost completely removed. Only if you listen very carefully can you still hear a short noise interfering with the harp sound in the lower frequencies. In some cases, this quick way of removing unwanted sound might be all you need. But Soundbooth can do even better than that. In a moment you will learn how you can extract sounds even if they are overlapping in frequencies with sounds that you do not want to delete. But before doing that, you'll learn how to undo (and redo) changes.

Using the Undo command and the History panel

While you are editing a sound file, Soundbooth keeps track of the commands you are performing. The modifications are not permanently applied to the file until you save the file and close it. If you make a mistake or want to experiment with different settings for a command, you can undo your changes and start all over again. Soundbooth offers two methods to step back through your list of performed commands, the Undo/Redo menu command and the History panel.

1 Choose Edit > Undo Delete Marquee Selection, or press Ctrl+Z (Windows) or Command+Z (Mac OS) to undo the silencing of the selected area. Your menu command might read Edit > Undo Apply Gain To Marquee Selection, depending on which method you used to silence the cough sound in step 7. For your convenience, the Undo command always indicates which change you're about to undo. At this time there are no more commands to be undone. The file is in the same state as when you opened it, and the Undo command is not available. However, the Redo command is now available to perform exactly the same modification to the file as before.

2   Choose Edit > Redo Delete Marquee Selection (or Edit > Redo Apply Gain To Marquee Selection), or press Ctrl+Y (Windows) or Command+Y (Mac OS) to redo the silencing of the selected area.

The Undo and Redo commands restrict you to an incremental sequence of changes. If you made many changes to a file and want to quickly revert back by several steps, use the History panel. The History panel lets you instantly revert back to any previous change, as well as redo a series of edits. That way you can use the History panel to quickly compare processed and original audio, or discard a series of changes that produced undesired results. At the moment, with the file you are now working on, there is only one command to undo and redo listed in the History panel, but the principle still applies.

3   In the History panel, click Open—listed as the first command—to revert to the file's original state.

4   Start playback to listen to the file in its original version.

5   In the History panel, click the last command listed—Delete Marquee Selection or Apply Gain To Marquee Selection—to redo all edits you have previously applied to the file.

6   Start playback to listen to the file in its modified version.

7   Click Open one more time in the History panel to prepare for the next exercise by reverting to the file's original state. Then, click anywhere in the spectral frequency display to clear the current selection.

> ♀ *With the History panel in focus, either press the up and down arrows on the keyboard, or choose Step Backward or Step Forward from the panel menu, to incrementally move through states. To delete a specific state, select it, and then click the trash icon located in the lower right corner of the History panel. To delete all states, choose Clear History from the panel menu. Deleting history states also removes related Undo commands.*

Visual healing

If you have used the healing brush tool in Adobe Photoshop you will immediately understand the advantage of Soundbooth's Auto Heal command over a simple Delete or Apply Gain command. Unlike the Delete command, which can introduce audible glitches, the Auto Heal command removes an unwanted sound and seamlessly blends the area with surrounding audio: A healing brush for sound. You'll be amazed when you see—and hear—the result.

1   Make sure you have the Open state selected in the History panel, so you start with the file in its original form.

2   If not already selected, select the Marquee tool in the Remove a Sound section of the Tasks panel.

3   Click and drag a marquee selection around the spectral representation of the cough. This time, also include the lower frequencies in the selection, as shown in the illustration below.

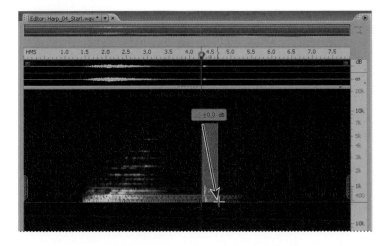

4   Choose Edit > Auto Heal, or click Auto Heal in the Remove a Sound section of the Tasks panel to heal the area selected in the spectral frequency display. The keyboard shortcut for the Auto Heal command is Ctrl+U (Windows) or Command+U (Mac OS).

The Applying effect dialog box is displayed briefly, and then the cough sound is magically removed from the selected area, leaving the harp sound and the slight background noise almost unaffected.

Note: The Auto Heal command can only be applied if the selection is not longer than 25,000 samples (0.52 seconds at a sample rate of 48 kHz). To precisely determine the selection length in sample units, right-click (Windows) or Control-click (Mac OS) the timeline ruler, and choose Samples from the context menu.

5   Click anywhere in the spectral frequency display to clear the current selection. Notice how well the edited area blends in visually. The slight noise in the higher frequencies remains almost unaffected and in the lower frequencies there is no longer any sudden spike visible where the cough sound was interfering with the harp sound.

6   Playback the file to confirm that it sounds as good as it looks.

7   Choose File > Save As. In the Save As dialog box, keeping the Windows Waveform file type selected, change the file name to **Harp_04_End.wav**, and then click Save to save the file in the Lesson04 folder on your hard disk. Click OK in the Save As Options dialog box without making any changes to the settings.

> 💡 *Soundbooth's auto healing functionality can also be utilized when performing other edit commands on selections. To automatically heal the outer edges of all edited selections, select Auto-Heal Edit Boundaries in the General section of the Preferences dialog box.*

8 (Optional) Close the file Harp_04_Start.wav without saving any changes.

Basic editing

In the last part of this lesson you'll learn about the most common editing tasks: trimming, silencing, fading, and normalizing.

Trimming

Most recordings have a few seconds of silence at either end. These extra seconds of silence are useful if you want to define a noise print before removing background noise throughout the recording. To prepare the sound file for use in another application like Adobe Premiere Pro, you would normally remove these leading and trailing seconds of silence; a process called trimming. Trimming is such a common editing task that Soundbooth offers on-clip trim handles to facilitate the process.

1 If not already selected, choose the file Harp_04_End.wav from the Files menu in the top left corner of the Editor panel to make it the current file.

2 If the spectral frequency display is visible, choose View > Spectral Frequency Display to close it. For this exercise, you'll perform the trimming in the waveform display even though the trim handles are also available in the spectral frequency display.

3 If necessary, click the Zoom Out Full button (🔍) located in the top right corner of the Editor panel, or choose View > Zoom Out Full, to display the entire section of audio and to reveal both trim handles at either end of the waveform display in the Editor panel.

4 In the waveform display of the Editor panel, position the cursor over the trim handle (│) at the beginning of the audio file. When the cursor changes to the red bracket with the black arrow pointing to the right (⊢), click and then drag the trim handle to the right. Release the pointer at about the 1.4 second mark. *(See illustration on next page.)*

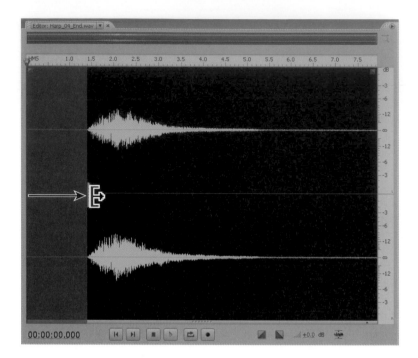

After you release the pointer, the silence at the beginning of the recording will be deleted.

💡 *Trimming is equivalent to deleting audio at the beginning or end of the file. To delete audio in the middle of a file, select the area you want to remove, and then choose Edit > Delete.*

Note: *When you edit audio from a video file, trim handles and the Delete command silence audio without changing the file length, maintaining synchronization with the video.*

5   Position the current-time indicator at the beginning of the file and press the spacebar to begin playback. Notice how the harp sound starts immediately. But at the end there's still a long silence that you will trim away next.

6   In the waveform display of the Editor panel, position the cursor over the trim handle at the end of the audio file ( ). When the cursor changes to the red bracket with the black arrow pointing to the left (◄), click and then drag the trim handle to the left. Release the pointer at about the 4 second mark.

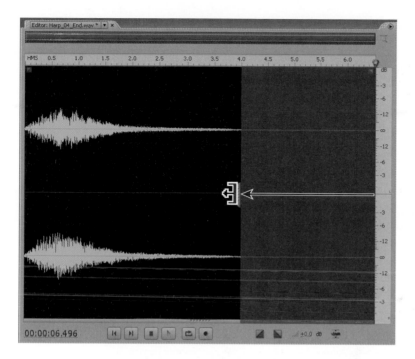

Inserting silence

The opposite of shortening a file by trimming or deleting a portion, is lengthening it by inserting silence. You might want to insert silence to either separate different types of program material, or to synchronize audio with a video file.

1   Position the current-time indicator at the beginning of the file (or any other location in the file where you want the inserted silence to begin).

2   Choose Edit > Insert Silence.

3   In the Insert Silence dialog box, enter the duration in seconds of the silence you want to insert, and then click OK.

Note: *If you don't see the Insert Silence dialog box, choose Edit > Undo Insert Silence, and then make sure you have no active selection before performing step 2. Otherwise, Insert Silence will silence the selected audio without affecting the file length.*

Applying a default fade in and fade out

If you trim the beginning or end of a song—for example to cut away unnecessarily long intros or trailings—you should apply a fade in or fade out so that the song does not start or end abruptly. At the bottom of the Editor panel, click the Fade In button or the Fade Out button.

A fade normally lasts several seconds. Since the file Harp_04_End.wav is hardly long enough to apply a fade, you'll be using the file Solace_04_End.wav for this exercise.

1   Choose the file Solace_04_End.wav from the Files menu in the top left corner of the Editor panel to make it the current file.

2   Use the trim handle to trim away the first half second of silence.

3   Click the Fade In button (■) located at the bottom of the Editor panel to apply a default 5-second fade at the start of the file.

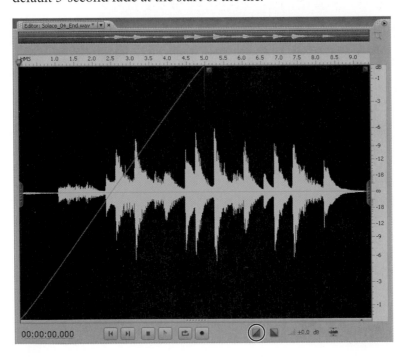

4   Click the Fade Out button (◣) located next to the Fade In button to apply a default 5-second fade at the end of the file.

5   Press the spacebar to start playback and notice how the volume slowly increases at the beginning and then decreases towards the end of the file.

Changing the fade duration and type

In some cases you might want to change the duration of the fade, or select a fade type that is exponential or logarithmic instead of linear.

1   To shorten the duration of the fade in, position the cursor over the Fade In handle (◼) located at the top of the waveform display. When the pointer changes to the hand icon (🖑), click and then drag the handle to the left. Release the pointer at approximately the 2 second mark.

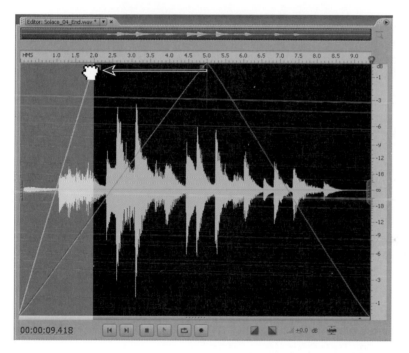

💡 *To come to the same result, you could have also dragged the Fade In handle inwards without first applying a default fade.*

2   (Optional) Shorten the duration of the fade out: Position the cursor over the Fade Out handle (◼) located at the top of the waveform display. When the pointer changes to the hand icon (🖑), click and then drag the handle to the right. Release the pointer at approximately the 7 second mark.

3   To change the fade in type, position the cursor over the Fade In handle (◼) located at the top of the waveform display. When the pointer changes to the hand icon (🖑), do one of the following:

- Click and then drag the handle downwards to create a long, smooth exponential fade.

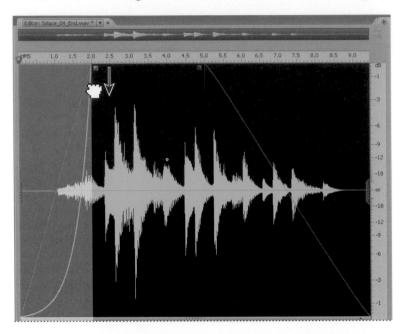

- Click and then drag the handle upwards to create a quick, smooth logarithmic fade.

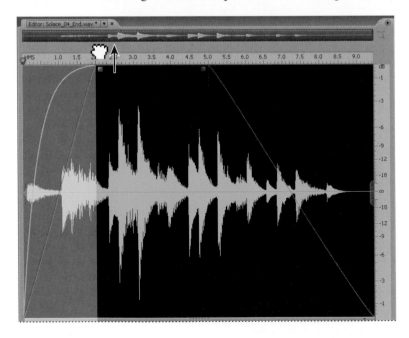

4 (Optional) To change the fade out type, position the cursor over the Fade Out handle (■) located at the top of the waveform display. When the pointer changes to the hand icon (☜), draw the handle up- or downwards to create the desired fade type, and then release the pointer.

💡 *Using the Fade In or Fade Out handles, you can change the duration and type of the fade at the same time by dragging sidewards as well as up- or downwards.*

5 Press the spacebar to start playback and notice the changed characteristic of the fade.

Changing the default fade type

You can select which fade type—linear, exponential, or logarithmic—is created when applying a default fade.

• Linear fades produce an even volume change that works well for most material.

• Exponential fades produce long, smooth fades that change volume at first slowly and then rapidly during fade ins, and at first rapidly and then slowly during fade outs.

• Logarithmic fades produce quick, smooth fades that change volume at first rapidly and then slowly during fade ins, and at first slowly and then rapidly during fade outs.

1 To select the fade type for the default fade in, right-click (Windows) or Control-click (Mac OS) the Fade In button, and then select a linear (◢), exponential (◢), or logarithmic (◢) fade type from the context menu that appears.

2 To select the fade type for the default fade out, right-click (Windows) or Control-click (Mac OS) the Fade Out button, and then select a linear (◣), exponential (◣), or logarithmic (◣) fade type from the context menu that appears.

Note: You can change the default fade type, but not the default fade duration of 5 seconds.

Adjusting volume

When you are done editing or applying effects (see Lesson 7, "Exploring Effects"), *normalizing* the volume gives the sound file the final touch. When normalizing, Soundbooth will proportionally increase the volume of the entire sound file—or the current selection—to just below the possible maximum without clipping the peak levels. Once the volume is normalized, you can choose to apply *hard limiting*, amplifying quieter sounds more than loud ones. Hard limiting increases the perceived volume but reduces the dynamic range of the recording.

1　With the file Solace_04_End.wav selected in the Editor panel, click once anywhere in the waveform display to clear any selection you might have.

2　Choose Edit > Make Louder, or click the Make Louder button (⊞) located at the bottom of the Editor panel.

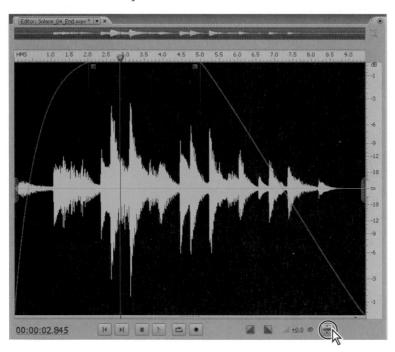

This will normalize the sound file, raising the volume to −0.3 dBFS (decibels full scale), just below the digital maximum, ensuring optimal volume while avoiding clipping. The peaks in the first half of the recording limit the effect of this process, resulting in only a slight increase of the overall volume.

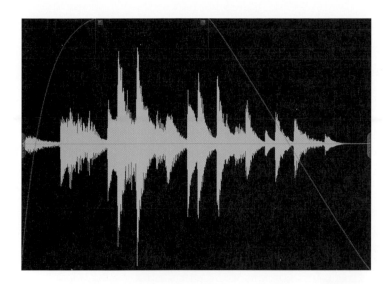

3   Choose Edit > Make Louder again, or click the Make Louder button (▦) a second time, to hard limit the audio, noticeably increasing the amplitude throughout the entire file yet not clipping the peaks.

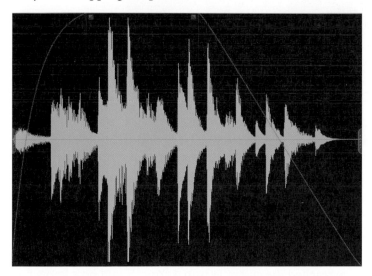

Each successive Make Louder command would increase overall volume by another 3 dB without clipping, while also reducing the dynamic range.

While the increase in volume is automatic when applying the Make Louder command, Soundbooth also lets you freely raise or lower the volume of a selected area.

4 Using the Time Selection tool, click and drag in the waveform display to select the area in which you would like to adjust the volume.

> 💡 *Double-click anywhere in the waveform display, or choose Edit > Select All to select the entire file.*

5 Position the cursor over the blue number in the volume pop-up bubble above the selected audio, or next to the volume icon ( ) at the bottom of the Editor panel. When the pointer changes to the hand with two arrows icon ( ), click and drag to the left to reduce or to the right to increase volume. The indicated volume change is applied when you release the pointer.

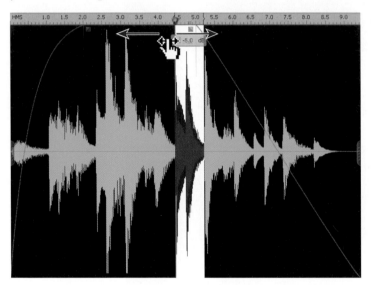

Note: While dragging, the blue numbers indicate the amount of amplitude change. When you release the pointer, the numbers return to 0 dB, so you can make further adjustments.

6 Save your changes and close all files.

Congratulations! You've reached the end of Lesson 4. You should now know how to remove noise or unwanted sounds from a recording—including using the powerful Auto Heal command, how to use the undo/redo commands and the History panel, and how to apply trims, fades, and volume adjustments. Take a moment to test your knowledge by working through the review questions and answers on the next page.

Review

▶ **Review questions**

1 What is a noise print?

2 Explain the Auto Heal function.

3 Name three common sound-editing tasks for which Soundbooth offers on-clip controls.

4 How do you delete audio in the middle of the file?

5 What does *hard limiting* mean?

▶ **Review answers**

1 A noise print can be used as reference when removing background noise from a recording. A noise print is best created from a section of the audio containing only noise. Creating a noise print is optional, but can help Soundbooth do a better job when removing noise.

2 The Auto Heal function works like the familiar Healing Brush in Photoshop, cleanly removing an unwanted sound while leaving desired audio intact. The Auto Heal function seamlessly blends the edited area with the surrounding audio.

3 You can trim a sound at either end using the trim handles, apply and modify fades using the Fade In and Fade Out handles, and adjust the volume of a selection by scrubbing the blue number in the volume pop-up bubble.

4 To delete audio in the middle of a file, select the area you want to remove, and then choose Edit > Delete.

5 Hard limiting is a way of increasing the perceived volume of a sound clip after it has been normalized. It increases the volume of quieter sounds more than the volume of louder sounds to avoid clipping of peak amplitudes.

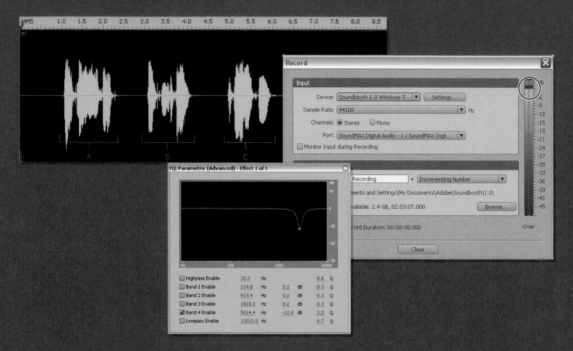

Use the Adobe Soundbooth CS3 Vocal Enhancer to automatically add the final polish to a track, or apply any of several professionally designed effects presets to enhance vocal tracks for more punch and clarity.

5 Editing and Enhancing Voiceover Recordings

Editing voice recordings in Soundbooth is comparable to using a word processor to edit written text. With some practice you can recognize individual words and phrases in the waveform display, and then use cut and paste commands to delete unwanted parts, or even rearrange the order of the words spoken. You then add emphasis to parts or all of the speech, much like you would choose a different font, change its size or color, or underline a word in a text document. Soundbooth offers various methods to make your voice recordings stand out.

In this lesson, you'll learn how to do the following:

- Record audio using a microphone.
- Edit voice recordings.
- Change Pitch and Timing.
- Apply Vocal Enhancer, Mastering, and EQ Effects.
- Use Rack Presets.

Before you begin, make sure that you have correctly copied the Lessons folder from the CD in the back of this book onto your computer's hard disk. See "Copying the Classroom in a Book files" on page 2.

Getting started

In this lesson, you'll learn how to record voice in Soundbooth using a microphone. You will then manipulate the recording by deleting unwanted parts, changing the order of words, adjusting pitch and timing, and applying effects for different sonic results.

Before you begin, perform the following steps to ensure that you start the lesson with the default window layout.

1 Start Adobe Soundbooth.

2 Select Window > Workspace > Default, if it is not already selected. Then, choose Window > Workspace > Reset "Default."

3 In the Reset Workspace dialog box, click OK.

Recording from a microphone

Soundbooth enables you to record sound from a wide range of hardware inputs, with a microphone being the method of choice for voice recordings. If your computer does not already come with a built-in microphone, then your sound card most likely possesses a line in or microphone port to connect an external microphone. There are also external microphones that you can connect via a USB port.

To work through the first part of this lesson, you need to have a microphone—either an internal or an external model—in working order, attached to your computer. Otherwise, you can still read through the instructions in this lesson even though you will not be able to make an actual voice recording. For your convenience, a voice recording that will be used later in the lesson is provided on the CD in the back of this book.

Adjusting the sound card's recording levels

Before you begin recording, you should confirm that your recording levels for your sound card are properly adjusted. If the recording levels are too low, the recording will be too quiet and contain too much background noise when normalized. If the recording levels are too high, the recording will be too loud and distorted. Soundbooth does not directly control the recording level of your sound card. If you are using a professional sound card, it will come with instructions on how to adjust these levels. For a standard sound card that comes built-in with your computer, you can use the control panels provided with the operating system.

1 To adjust the sound card levels for recording in Mac OS, do the following:

• From the Apple menu, choose System Preferences.

- Type **sound input level** in the search field located in the top right corner of the System Preferences dialog box, and then press enter or return.

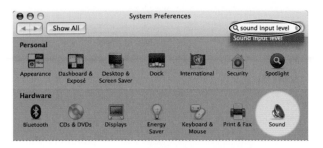

- Select Internal microphone as sound input if you want to use the built-in microphone, or Line In if you want to use an external microphone plugged into the audio line-in port. Then, while talking into the microphone, adjust the Input volume slider until you see a good response in the Input level meter. For best results, the peak meter reading should be in the range of ⅔ to ¾ full.

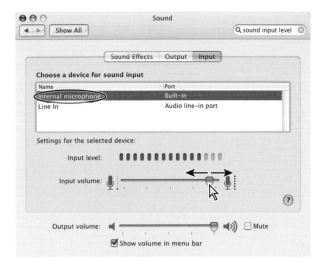

2   To adjust the sound card levels for recording on Windows XP, do the following:

- Click the Start button in the taskbar, and then choose Control Panel.

- When in Category View, select the Sounds, Speech, and Audio Devices category, and then open the Sounds and Audio Devices control panel. *(See illustration on next page.)*

• When in Classic View, find and open the Sounds and Audio Devices control panel.

• In the Sounds and Audio Devices Properties control panel, select the Audio tab. Under Sound recording, select the audio mixer device from the menu, and then click the Volume button located below the menu.

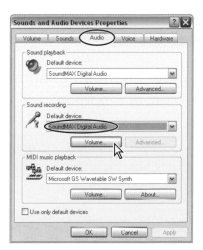

• In the Recording Control control panel, select the sound input channel you want to use. Adjust the input level with the Volume slider.

• To test your settings, watch the level meters in Soundbooth's Record dialog box (see "Recording a new file" on the next page). Try to adjust the input level so that the loudest peaks stay in the yellow range, below -3 dB.

Recording a new file

1   To start recording a new file, open the Record dialog box by choosing File > Record or clicking the Record button (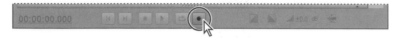) in the Editor panel.

Note: The Record button in the Editor panel is not available when working with scores (See Lesson 6, "Creating Background Music"). Either close the score first, or use the menu command File > Record to start a new recording.

2   In the Record dialog box, test the input levels by speaking into the microphone and watching the level meters on the right side of the dialog box. Make sure that the sound levels approach 0 dB as closely as possible without entering the red area.

Note: If you aren't seeing any signal in the level meter, it might be necessary to configure the input device. Select the driver for your input device from the Device menu. If a driver isn't available for your device, select Soundbooth 1.0 Windows Sound (Windows) or System Default Input/Output (Mac OS). Click Settings to open a dialog in which you can adjust the settings for your input device. The exact settings you need depend on your audio hardware.

3   Choose a sample rate from the Sample Rate menu, or accept the default of 44,100 Hz (samples per second), the sample rate used for audio CDs.

4   Enter a file name and choose a name extension option for consecutive recordings from the menu next to the File Name text field.

5　Get ready to start speaking. Click the Record button (⬤) located near the lower left corner of the Record dialog box, wait for about one second, and then read the following text:

> *While playing in the park,*
> *I threw the ball.*
> *The ball I threw,*
> *has not yet reached the ground.*

6　When finished reading, wait about one second, and then click the Stop button (⬛) located next to the Record button.

> 💡 *While recording, you can click the Add Marker button (⬛) to add audio markers at specific points in time. You'll learn more about markers in Lesson 8, "Working with Markers."*

7　(Optional) Repeat steps 5 and 6 if you want to make additional recordings of these lines.

8　When done recording, click the Close button located at the bottom of the dialog box to close the Record dialog box.

Soundbooth stores your recording in WAV format in the specified location, and displays its waveform in the Editor panel. Your waveform display should look similar to the one shown in the illustration below.

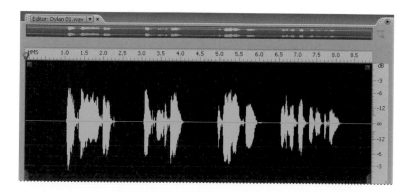

Identifying words in a voice recording

Before you can make changes to recorded speech, like changing the order of words or deleting unwanted parts, you need to identify the waveform patterns corresponding to the spoken words. For the remainder of this lesson you can either try to use the recording you just made, or use the voice recording provided on the CD.

1   To use the voice recording provided on the CD, choose File > Open. In the Open Files dialog box that appears, navigate to your Lesson05 folder you copied to your hard disk. Within that folder, select the file Dylan_05.wav, and then click Open.

2   Press the spacebar to start playback. Listen to the recording a few times, watching the current-time indicator as it is passing through the waveform. This should give you a rough idea what part of the waveform forms which part of the sentence.

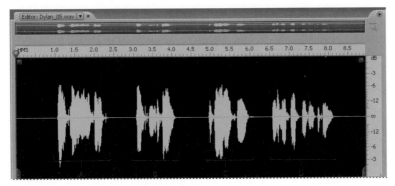

Waveform patterns of recorded speech:
A. *"While playing in the park,"* **B.** *"I threw the ball."* **C.** *"The ball I threw,"* **D.** *"Has not yet reached the ground."*

To better determine word boundaries, you'll use another technique. You'll focus on the last sentence, and scrub the current-time indicator back and forth while listening for word boundaries.

3   Using the Time Selection tool from the Tools panel, click and drag to select the last sentence in the waveform display (from approximately the 6.5 second mark to the 8.2 second mark in the file Dylan_05.wav provided on the CD). Then, choose View > Zoom To Selection.

4   Click anywhere in the waveform display to clear the current selection.

5   Click in the timeline ruler, and then drag the current-time indicator back and forth over parts of the waveform. While doing so, try to identify the word boundaries in the waveform.

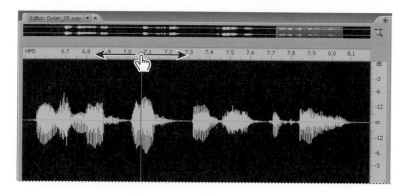

With a little bit of practice, you'll be able to precisely identify the boundaries of waveform patterns corresponding to the words spoken.

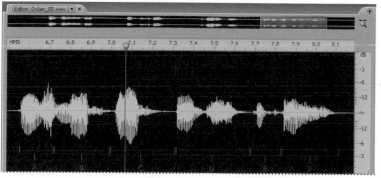

Identifying word boundaries:
A. *"Has"* ***B.*** *"not"* ***C.*** *"yet"* ***D.*** *"reached"* ***E.*** *"the"* ***F.*** *"ground."*

Once you've identified sentence and word boundaries in your waveform, you can cut and paste sections of the waveform to rearrange the word order—almost like in a word processor application. Deleting or rearranging the order of complete sentences is the easiest. It is harder to cut within sentences. Try to avoid cutting on vowels and soft sounds like 'S.' These cuts are easily noticed. For best results, look for consonants and plosives like 'K,' 'T,' 'B,' 'P,' and 'Ch' to cut on.

In the following exercise, you will delete the "I threw the ball" part of the first sentence and move the "The ball I threw" part of the second sentence to the very beginning.

Cutting and pasting within a voice recording

You will now arrange the words in the recording to form the last sentence of the poem *Should Lanterns Shine* by Dylan Thomas:

> *The ball I threw while playing in the park*
> *Has not yet reached the ground.*

1   To see the entire voice recording in the Editor panel, do one of the following:

• Click the Zoom Out Full button (⬚) located in the top right corner of the Editor panel.

• Choose View > Zoom Out Full.

• Use the keyboard shortcut backslash key (\\).

2   Using the Time Selection tool, select the second part of the recording—the "I threw the ball" part, which ranges from around the 2.8 second mark to the 4.5 second mark in the file Dylan_05.wav.

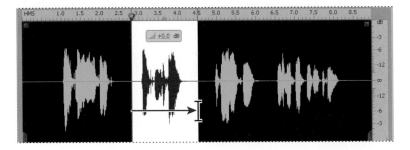

3   Choose Edit > Delete. The selection is deleted from the file and the parts following the selection move to the left to fill the gap. You would use the same technique to delete unwanted occurrences of *um* or *hmm* in a voice recording.

4   Using the Time Selection tool, select the part immediately following the deleted section—the "The ball I threw" part.

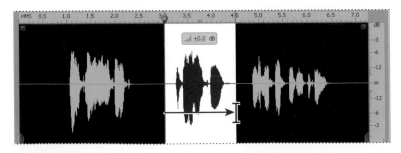

5   To listen to the selection, select Loop Playback (▣), and then click Play (▶) in the group of transport controls at the bottom of the Editor panel. Click Stop (▪) when you are sure that you have selected the correct section.

6   Choose Edit > Cut to delete the selection from the file while saving a copy to the clipboard. In the next step you will insert the content of the clipboard near the beginning of the file.

7   Position the current-time indicator somewhere in the silent part at the beginning of the file, and then choose Edit > Paste.

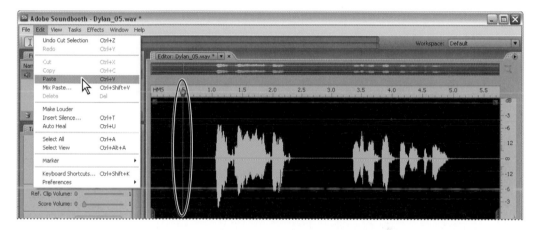

💡 *You can cut and paste between different files. For example, if you made several recordings of the same text, you can pick and choose the best parts of each and mix them together in a new file.*

8   Position the current-time indicator at the beginning of the file, and then press the spacebar to start playback. While listening, pay attention to the length of the silent parts. If you think a pause is too long, select a small area of that silence, and then choose Edit > Delete. To extend the length of a pause, position the current-time indicator where you want to add some silence, choose Edit > Insert Silence, and specify the duration in the Insert Silence dialog box.

9   When done editing, choose File > Save to save your changes.

Changing pitch and timing

At times you may want to adjust the length of a voiceover to fit perfectly to the length of a video scene or an animation, while maintaining speech characteristics, or change the pitch of the voice with or without changing the length of the recording. These modifications are usually referred to as *time stretching* and *pitch shifting*. They are such common sound-editing tasks that Soundbooth features a dedicated Change Pitch and Timing task.

1   In the Tasks panel, click Change Pitch and Timing, or choose Tasks > Change Pitch and Timing.

2   Select the area of the waveform you would like to modify, or clear the selection to work on the entire file. Then, click the Pitch and Timing button under Change Pitch and Timing in the Tasks panel to open the Pitch and Timing dialog box.

3   In the Pitch and Timing dialog box, do any or all or the following:

•   To stretch or shorten the audio to a specific length, adjust the value for New Duration by either dragging the blue number, or clicking it to enter a specific time.

•   Drag the Time Stretch or Pitch Shift sliders, or adjust the corresponding blue numbers to change the audio relative to its current value. For example, slide the Time Stretch slider to 90% to reduce the total length by 10%, or enter **-1** as value for Pitch Shift to lower the pitch by 1 unit—the musical interval of a semitone, or half-step.

4   To hear how your modifications would affect the sound—without yet committing the changes to the file—click the Preview button located in the lower left corner of the Pitch and Timing dialog box.

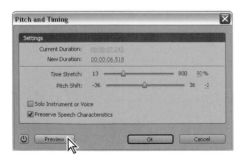

A Rendering dialog box appears before playback begins—rendering time depends on the length of your file or selection.

5   When done listening, click the same button again—the text on that button changes to Stop during playback—to stop preview.

6   Click to toggle the Power button between active (◉) and inactive (◉) to compare processed and original audio during playback.

7   Experiment with selecting or deselecting the Solo Instruments or Voice, or the Preserve Speech Characteristics option, to find the results that sound best for your purpose.

8   When ready, click OK to process the audio file according to your settings and to close the dialog box.

9   Using the Time Selection tool, click anywhere in the waveform display to clear the selection, position the current-time indicator at the start of the file, and then press spacebar to listen to your modifications applied to the file. Press the spacebar again to stop playback.

10   Choose File > Save to save your changes.

Applying the Vocal Enhancer effect

Unless you are a trained voiceover artist and have access to a professional recording studio, your voice recordings will most likely suffer from artifacts like sibilants and plosives. *Sibilants* are high-frequency hissing sounds, produced when pronouncing words containing, for example, 's', 'ch', or 'z.' *Plosives* are popping sounds, produced when pronouncing words containing, for example, 'p', 't', or 'd.' You can try to minimize the problems caused by sibilants and plosives through the use of high-quality recording equipment, proper placement of the microphone, and vocal training of the speaker. In most cases, though, you will have to deal with sub-optimal recordings. Soundbooth offers an easy to use vocal enhancer effect, to quickly improve the quality of a voiceover recording by reducing sibilance and plosives, as well as microphone handling noise.

1   Using the Time Selection tool, click anywhere in the waveform display to clear any selection you might have active. You would normally want to apply the vocal enhancer effect to the entire length of the recording spoken by one person.

Note: For best results, make pitch and time shift corrections only before and not after applying effects like the vocal enhancer effect. Otherwise, subtle artifacts that are usually not noticeable could become amplified and possibly disturbing. As the last step before applying the Vocal Enhancer effect, normalize the file by using the Make Louder button.

2   Choose Effects > Vocal Enhancer. The Effects panel will come forward, and the Vocal Enhancer effect is added to the Effects Rack. For the moment, don't worry too much about all the buttons you can click in the Effects panel and menus you can select from the Effects menu. You will learn more about applying and customizing Effects and the Effects panel—including the Effects Rack and Stereo Rack Presets—later in this lesson, as well as in Lesson 7, "Exploring Effects."

3   If not already active, select Loop Playback (⬚) in the Editor panel, and then click Play (▶) to start playback.

4   In the Effects panel, select—one after the other—Default, Female, Male, and finally Music from the Effect Preset menu of the Vocal Enhancer effect. Try to notice the slight variation in tone that each of these settings produces. The Default setting, by the way, turns the Vocal Enhancer effect off, thus leaving the voice unchanged. The Female and Male settings try to improve the audio for a typical female and male voice, respectively. Results vary depending on the characteristics of the recorded voice. Rest assured that there are many more effects and presets to experiment with—and almost unlimited possibilities to customize their settings—to find just the right solution for your needs. The Music setting—to complete the list—is intended to tone down music or background audio to better complement a foreground voiceover.

5 Click Stop (■) to stop playback.

6 As preparation for the next exercise, choose Effects > Remove All Effects, to remove the Vocal Enhancer effect—or any other effect you might have accidentally added—from the Effects Rack.

Mastering and advanced mastering

Mastering normally refers to the final optimization of the sound file for the intended output media. For example, if you expect the sound to be played on tiny computer speakers that badly reproduce low frequencies, you can boost these frequencies when mastering to compensate for output media deficiencies. Some of Soundbooth's Mastering effects can also be used to improve you voiceover recording in general, or to apply some interesting effects.

1 Right-click (Windows) or Control-click (Mac OS) in the Effects panel, and then choose Mastering from the context menu.

2 Choose Vocal Touch Up - Mild from the Effect Preset menu of the Mastering effect. Press the spacebar to start playback. You should notice a slight improvement—a fuller, richer voice.

3 Click to toggle the Power button next to Mastering between active (⊙) and inactive (⊙), to compare processed and original audio during playback.

4 Stop playback when you're done comparing. Before continuing to the next steps, be sure to reset the Power button next to Mastering to active (◉).

5 You can add more than one effect to the Effects Rack, or even multiple copies of the same effect. Right-click (Windows) or Control-click (Mac OS) in the Effects panel, and then choose Mastering from the context menu to add a second instance of the Mastering effect to the Effects Rack. This time, choose Bright Excitement - Mild from the Effect Preset menu. This will add crispness and clarity to the voice.

6 Press the spacebar to start playback. Click to toggle the Power button next to either effect, to compare the audio with and without this particular effect being applied. Click to toggle the Power Button located in the lower left corner of the Effects panel to compare original audio (no effect applied) with processed audio (all effects applied with active Power button in the Effects Rack).

7 Stop playback when you're done comparing. Be sure to reset all three Power buttons to active (◉) before continuing with the next steps.

If you find yourself using two or more copies of the same effect to achieve the desired result, you're probably better off using one instance of the advanced version of that effect and adjusting its settings accordingly.

Note: *The only effect without an advanced version is the Vocal Enhancer effect.*

8   Choose Effects > Remove All Effects, and then choose Effects > Advanced > Mastering (Advanced). From the Mastering (Advanced) Effect Preset menu choose Subtle Clarity.

9   Click Settings to open the Mastering (Advanced) options panel.

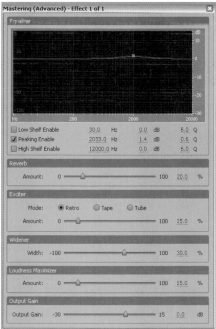

The Subtle Clarity effect preset uses the following settings:

- In the Equalizer, the frequencies around 2000 Hz are slightly amplified. The *voice frequency spectrum*, a band roughly between 300 Hz and 3 kHz, contains most of the audio that affects the intelligibility of speech. You would want to emphasis these frequencies for a voice recording, or tone them down for background audio to better complement a foreground voiceover.

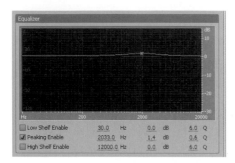

💡 *You can also have voice stand out by lowering the amplitudes above and below the voice frequency spectrum, as done in the Vocal Emphasis preset of the EQ: Graphic effect.*

- Reverb adds echoes as if the audio is reflected from walls, creating ambience and giving the voice more volume.

- The Exciter adds and amplifies harmonics in the high frequencies, making the voice sound bright and crisp. As Mode, choose Retro for a slight distortion, Tape for bright tones, or Tube for a quick, dynamic response.

- Drag the Widener slider to the left to increase the central focus of the sound. When set to -100, the Widener effectively converts from stereo to mono. Positive values increase the spatial distance between individual sound sources.

10 Without closing the Mastering (Advanced) options panel, choose Bright Hype from the Mastering (Advanced) Effect Preset menu to display its settings.

 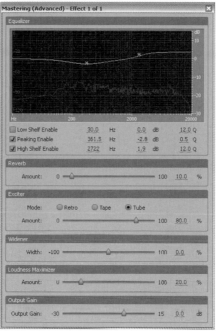

The Bright Hype effect preset uses a different equalizer curve, a slightly lower Reverb value, and a much higher Exciter value. Starting from an effect preset that comes closest to your intended effect, you can adjust each of the settings further to optimize your results.

11 (Optional) To listen to a more extreme example of what is possible by adjusting the settings of the Mastering (Advanced) effect, choose Dream Sequence from the Mastering (Advanced) Effect Preset menu, and then start playback.

12 Close the Mastering (Advanced) options panel by clicking its Close button (☒).

13 Right-click (Windows) or Control-click (Mac OS) the Mastering (Advanced) effect in the Effects Rack, and then choose Remove Selected Effects from the context menu.

Sibilants revisited

If you didn't quite get rid of the sibilants in your recording using the Vocal Enhancer effect earlier in this lesson, here's your chance to deal with this problem using the EQ: Parametric (Advanced) effect.

1   With the Effects Rack empty and your voice recording open in the Editor panel, click the Add Effect button (🎛️) located in the lower right corner of the Effects panel, and then choose Advanced > EQ: Parametric (Advanced) from the menu.

2   Choose Sibilant Attenuation from the Effect Preset menu of the EQ: Parametric (Advanced) effect.

3   Using the Time Selection tool, select in the Editor panel a section of the waveform that contains a hissing 's' sound, as in the word *reached* near the end of the file Dylan_ 05.wav.

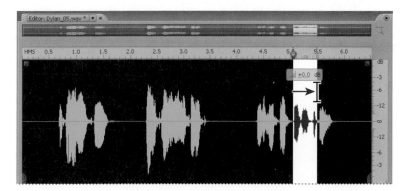

4   Choose View > Spectral Frequency Display. Notice the increased amplitudes (indicated by brighter colors) in the higher frequencies of the selected area—the hissing 's' sound. Sibilants usually appear in the frequency range from about 2 to 5 kHz, but the exact sibilance frequency varies greatly from person to person.

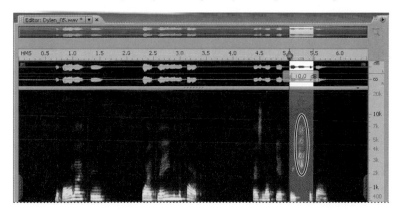

5   Click Settings to open the EQ: Parametric (Advanced) options panel.

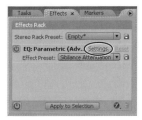

6   Arrange the EQ: Parametric (Advanced) options panel on the screen so that you can see it and the selected area in the Editor panel at the same time. Drag the current-time indicator in the timeline, going back and forth over the area with the hissing sound. In the equalizer display of the EQ: Parametric (Advanced) options panel, notice the amplitude peaks in the 2 to 6 kHz range—just below the band around 8 kHz, where the Sibilance Attenuation default preset reduces the amplitudes.

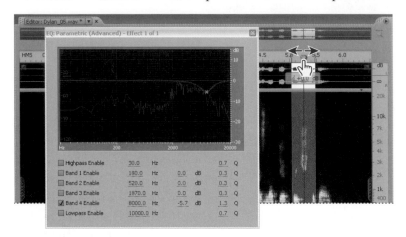

7   With Loop Playback enabled, press the spacebar to start playback. While listening to the processed sound, drag the cross on the red curve in the equalizer display to the left and slightly down, to lower the center frequency and to increase the level of amplitude reduction for band 4. While dragging, listen to the processed sound to find the best setting. You don't want to remove the hissing sound completely, but tone it down noticeably. We used the values 4632 Hz and -12.4 dB. You can enter these values directly in the blue numbers for Band 4.

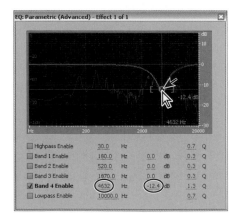

8   To increase the width of the affected frequency band, decrease the Q value. We used a Q value of 0.5. Notice the change in the form of the red curve, which is now less steep.

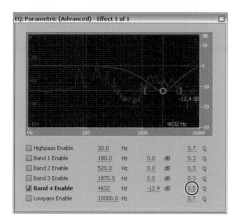

9   Close the EQ: Parametric (Advanced) options panel by clicking its Close button (⊠).

10   With the current selection still active in the Editor panel, click the Apply to Selection button (⌜Apply to Selection⌟) located at the bottom of the Effects panel. The effect is processed and the waveform modified. In the spectral frequency display, notice the reduction of high amplitudes (resulting in less bright colors) in the high frequencies of the selected area.

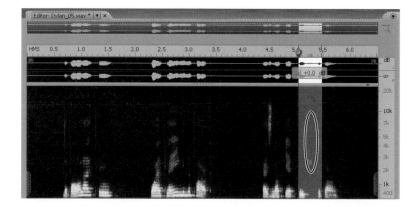

Note: The Effects Rack is now empty. The effects have been applied to the selection and the waveform is modified.

11 Clear the selection in the waveform display, position the current-time indicator at the beginning of the file, and then press the spacebar to start playback. Notice how the hissing 's' sound is removed from the word *reached* (but is still present in the word *has*).

12 Close the spectral frequency display (removing the checkmark from the View > Spectral Frequency Display menu), and then choose File > Save to save your changes. You are now ready for the last exercise.

Using effects rack presets

Effects rack presets are similar to effect presets. But instead of specifying the settings for just one effect, you can save—and restore—the settings of all effects in the effects rack at the same time. You can add up to five effects to the effects rack. You'll learn more about effect presets and effects rack presets in Lesson 7, "Exploring Effects." In this lesson, you will simply apply some of the effects rack presets that are relevant for editing voice.

1 In the Effects panel, click the triangle in the menu next to Stereo Rack Preset to see the long list of predefined Stereo Rack Presets. At the end of that list (shortened in the illustration below) you'll find presets especially defined for working with voice recordings. The menu names of these presets begin with the prefix "Voice: ."

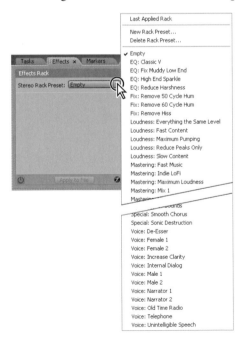

2   Let's start with the first preset and see what it does: Choose Voice: De-Esser from the Stereo Rack Preset menu.

One effect, the EQ: Parametric (Advanced) effect, is added to the Effects Rack. If you click on Settings you'll see the EQ: Parametric (Advanced) options panel you're already familiar with from the last exercise. Notice that the settings differ slightly from the ones used in the Sibilant Attenuation effect preset. While this may not seem to be a very exciting introduction to effects rack presets, it illustrates two things: Firstly, an effects rack preset can consist of only one effect (although you could get the same result using a simple effect preset), and secondly, the individual settings of an effect are specified by the effects rack preset.

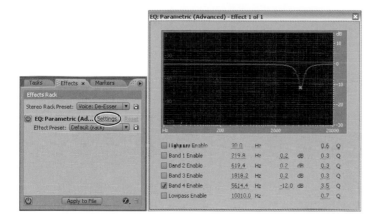

By defining effects rack presets with a common menu name prefix, you can group all your customized presets—using one or multiple effects—in one menu location.

3   Next, choose Voice: Female 1 from the Stereo Rack Preset menu. EQ: Parametric (Advanced) effect is cleared from the rack, and replaced by two other effects, the EQ: Graphic effect and the Dynamics (Advanced) effect.

4   Choose, in turn, all the rack presets with the "Voice: " name prefix. Listen to their effect on the recording.

5   For some special effects, select some of the presets with the "Special: " name prefix—some of them using the maximum of five effects in the effects rack.

6   You might like to experiment with the other presets as well. Click on Settings in the individual effects to access their effect options panels. Experiment with their settings. When you're done, either save the file with an effect you particularly like, or close the file without saving.

Sit back and relax! You've reached the end of a long lesson, filled with an enormous amount of information on working with voice recordings. You started off by setting up your sound input levels and recording voice using a microphone. Then you learned how to identify spoken words in the waveform, and how to cut and paste in a voice recording. You learned about time stretching and pitch shifting, sibilants and plosives, and various simple and advanced effects used to improve sound. You should now be well prepared to breeze through the review questions and answers on the next page.

Review

▶ **Review questions**

1 How can you remove unwanted occurrences of *um* or *hmm* in a voice recording?

2 Why would you want to make multiple recordings of the same text?

3 What are sibilants and plosives?

4 What is the voice frequency spectrum?

5 What is a De-Esser and how does it work?

▶ **Review answers**

1 First you identify in the waveform display—for example by scrubbing with the current-time indicator over the timeline—the boundaries of the waveform corresponding to the unwanted sound snippet. Then, you can select the section and choose Edit > Delete to remove it.

2 With multiple recordings of the same text, you can use the cut and paste commands to pick and choose the best parts of each recording and combine them in a new file.

3 *Sibilants* are high-frequency hissing sounds, produced when pronouncing words containing, for example, 's', 'ch', or 'z'. *Plosives* are popping sounds, produced when pronouncing words containing, for example, 'p', 't', or 'd'.

4 The voice frequency spectrum, a band roughly between 300 Hz and 3 kHz, contains most of the audio that affects the intelligibility of speech. You would want to emphasis these frequencies for a voice recording, or tone them down for background audio to better complement a foreground voiceover.

5 A De-Esser reduces the amount of hissing 's' sounds in a voice recording. It does so by selectively reducing the amplitude of the audio in the high frequencies.

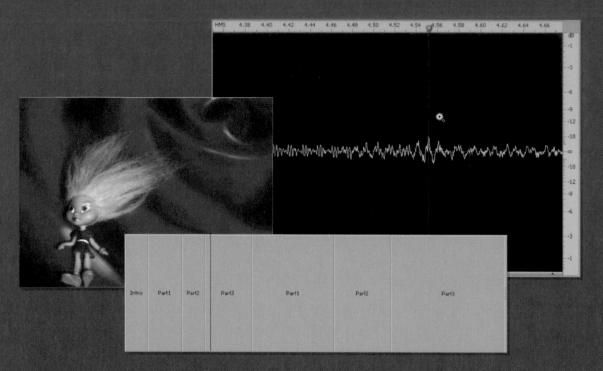

Easily produce customized music for your projects with the AutoComposer and a library of score templates created by professional musicians. Stretch music automatically to match the length of your video clip, and adjust intensity to match the mood.

6 | Creating Background Music

Creating or finding the right background music that reflects the mood of your work without detracting from the visuals is always a challenging task, especially if you're not a musician.

Soundbooth offers two quick solutions to create and fine-tune scores to perfectly fit your Flash animations, video projects or slide shows. The intuitive AutoComposer includes a library of professional-sounding, royalty-free scores that enable you to quickly customize your chosen piece of music by using a series of slider controls. As an alternative, you can work on the perfect sound track by creating loops of parts of a score—here, the Auto-Smooth Loop Point option comes in handy for seamless transitions in between loops.

In this lesson, you will learn how to do the following:

- Select an AutoComposer score template.
- Use the AutoComposer.
- Add a video clip for reference.
- Refine and customize an AutoComposer score.
- Animate a score with keyframes.
- Determine the length of a loop.
- Create a loop.
- Use the Auto-Smooth Loop option.

Before you begin, make sure that you have correctly copied the Lessons folder from the CD in the back of this book onto your computer's hard disk. See "Copying the Classroom in a Book files" on page 2.

Getting started

Perform the following steps to ensure that you start the lesson with the default window layout.

1   Start Adobe Soundbooth.

2   Select Window > Workspace > Default, if it is not already selected. Then, choose Window > Workspace > Reset "Default."

3   In the Reset Workspace dialog box, click OK.

Creating scores with the AutoComposer

The AutoComposer is a brilliant feature that enables you to easily customize the length, intensity and volume of a music score. Soundbooth offers dozens of precomposed scores templates. You can customize these score templates to suit your project perfectly.

These score templates are modular, consisting of beginning, middle, and end parts that are flexible, to match the length of the related video clip. You can change the overall feel of a score with the help of sliders. All the supplied scores are played and composed by accomplished musicians, and for maximum quality they are provided in uncompressed WAV format. It's definitely worthwhile listening to all these templates, as their melodies and moods can give you inspiration for your visuals.

Choose a score template and add a video clip for reference

1   In the Tasks panel, click AutoCompose Score.

2   To browse for a score template (*.sbst) file using Adobe Bridge, click Browse Scores.

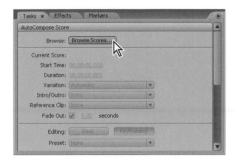

3 In Adobe Bridge, navigate to your Lesson06 folder that you copied to your hard disk. Within that folder, double-click the Aquo Visit folder icon to show that folder's content in the Content view of Bridge.

4 Within the Aquo Visit folder, double-click the AquoVisit.sbst file icon to open this score template in Soundbooth.

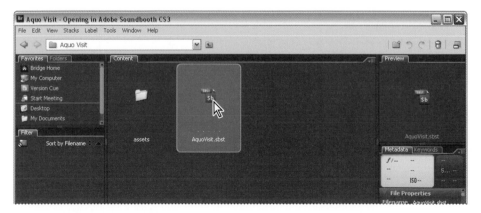

5 To listen to the AutoComposer score template that you just opened, click the Play button (![icon]) in the group of transport control buttons at the bottom of the Editor panel.

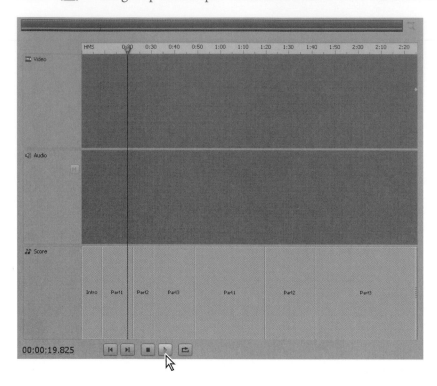

In the next steps you will open—as a reference—the video file for which the score is to be customized.

6 In the Tasks panel under AutoCompose Score, notice that the menu for the Reference Clip is currently disabled. You need to load a file into the Files panel before it can be selected from the Reference Clip menu.

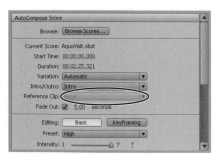

7 Choose File > Open. In the Open Files dialog box, navigate to the Lesson06 folder. Within that folder, select the video file Flowerdolls.mp4, and then click Open.

Note: *If you don't see the filename or the filename is grayed out, choose All Supported Media from the Files of type (Windows) or Enable (Mac OS) menu.*

8 Using the files menu located in the top left corner of the Editor panel, switch back to the file AquoVisit.sbst. Notice that in the AutoCompose Score section of the Tasks panel the Reference Clip menu is now enabled. Choose the file Flowerdolls.mp4 from that menu.

9 In the Editor panel you see the video being displayed in the video track with its audio track and the AutoComposer score track below. The score template has not yet been modified, hence the length does not match the length of the video clip. In the next step, you will shorten the score to match the length of the video. The Audio track is empty, as the video does not include sound or voiceover. If not already visible, open the Video panel (Window > Video). If necessary, adjust the size of the Video panel, and then click the Play button (⏵) in the group of transport control buttons at the bottom of the Editor panel. *(See illustration on the next page.)*

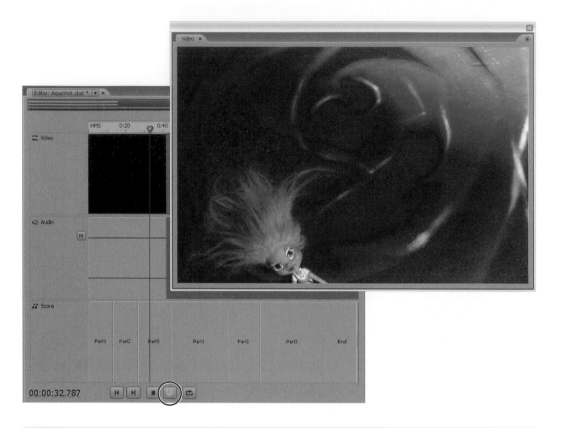

💡 *If you prefer using the predefined workspace for editing scores for a video, choose Window > Workspace > Edit Score to Video.*

Modifying the length of the AutoComposer score

The settings for score length and other characteristics such as the intensity can be quickly adjusted to fit to your audio, video, or Flash projects.

In some cases, one of the predefined durations of the score might fit perfectly. Those presets, defined by the composer with an ideal order of musical arrangements, can be found under the Variation menu. But for our project, a custom score length is needed.

1   In the Editor panel, position the pointer over the right edge of the score track. When the pointer changes to the double-arrow icon (◀▶), click and drag the right edge to the left. Release the pointer when the right edge of the score aligns roughly with the end of the video clip, near the 42 second mark.

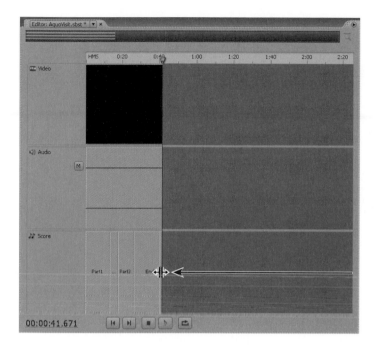

💡 *To change the start time of the score, you can adjust the Start Time value in the AutoCompose Score section of the Tasks panel. Or, click the middle of the score—anywhere in the score except over the right edge—and then drag to reposition it.*

2   For a perfect match, you can look up the exact length of the video clip in the Files panel (you might have to scroll to the right to locate the Duration column), and then enter the same value (**00:00:41.775** in this case) as Duration in the AutoCompose Score section of the Tasks panel.

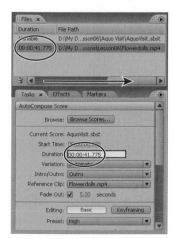

3 From the Intro/Outro menu, choose Outro. Leave Fade Out selected, accepting its default length of 5 seconds.

4 To play the customized score, press the spacebar.

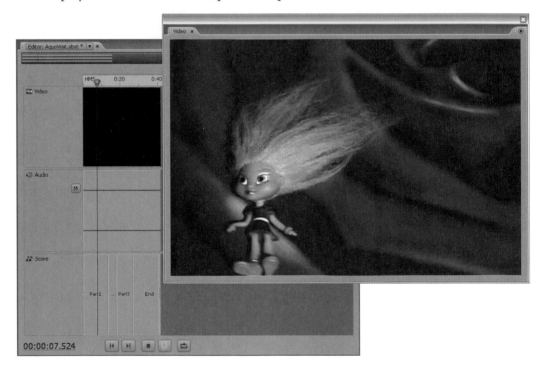

Overall, the combination of images and sound is already pretty good. It's always surprising how much the right background music can add to an animation or video project. You will now even better match this score to the images by experimenting with the intensity of the score.

Customizing the overall character of the AutoComposer score

The overall feel of the AutoComposer score can be modified. You are able to quickly make these adjustments by choosing from the Preset menu, an option that gets applied once it is selected. To fine-tune your score even further, AutoComposer offers sliders to change its parameters. By default, the Intensity is set to High. Let's now just check out what a lower intensity sounds like.

1   In the AutoCompose Score section of the Tasks panel, select Medium-Low from the Intensity menu.

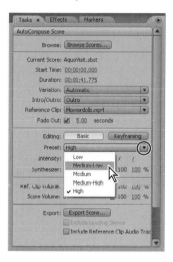

2   Press the spacebar to listen to the altered score. It is amazing how different it sounds. Next will be to animate the score with keyframes, so that part of the score will feel less intense, while the rest of the score will maintain a high intensity.

Animate scores with keyframes

The use of keyframes enables you to create dynamic musical scores, meaning that you can increase the dramatic effect, or change the mood of a score at a specific point in time. For example, you can gradually intensify the score by adding an Intensity keyframe with the value of 1 at the beginning of a composition, and one with the value of 10 at the end.

Soundbooth automatically calculates all the intermediate values, using one of the following two transition methods:

- Hold (■) transitions create an abrupt change in value at each new keyframe.

- Linear (◆) transitions create a smooth, gradual change between keyframes.

To change the type of keyframe, right-click (Windows) or Control-click (Mac OS) the keyframe, and then choose Linear or Hold from the context menu.

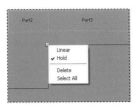

In the following exercise you will apply a Hold transition for the start of Part 3 of the score starts.

1   To enable the keyframe animation, click Keyframing in the AutoCompose Score section of the Tasks panel.

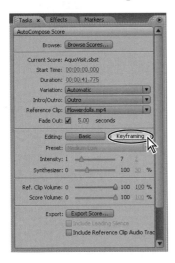

2   Choose View > Zoom In or View > Zoom Out Full to better see the individual parts of the score in the Editor panel.

3   Position the current-time indicator at the beginning of the score, and then click the Add/Remove Keyframe icon (◆) next to Intensity in the Editor panel. Notice the keyframe added in the Intensity track at the beginning of the score.

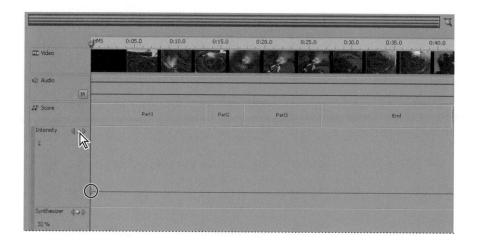

Note: *To delete a keyframe, right-click (Windows) or Control-click (Mac OS) the keyframe, and then choose Delete from the context menu. Or, use the arrow icons next to the Add/ Remove Keyframe icon to position the current-time indicator over the keyframe you want to delete, and then click the Add/Remove Keyframe icon.*

4 To add a second Hold keyframe, position the current-time indicator at the beginning of Part 3 of the score (at approximately the 17.6 second mark), and then click the Add/Remove keyframe icon again.

5 Drag the second keyframe up to increase the intensity (one step from the top is Intensity level 6, which is a good value for our purpose). When you release the pointer, notice that the blue line indicating the Intensity level now makes an abrupt change in value at the second keyframe.

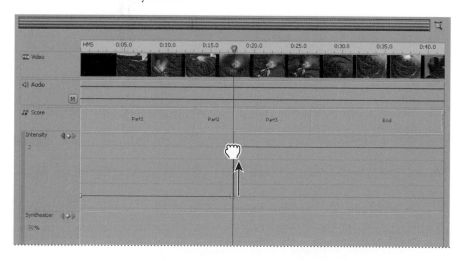

6 Press the spacebar to again listen to the score.

The score starts out with less intense acoustical instruments and ends with much more intense amplified instruments. The intensity can be further fine-tuned by changing the parameters for synthesizers or volume. Keyframes are great to add drama and life to your score. In Lesson 9, "Importing, Exporting, and Round-trip Editing," you will learn how to export a score in different file formats.

💡 *Access Resource Central online from within Adobe Soundbooth CS3 (Window > Resource Central) to quickly add scores or sound effects to your visual production. Resource Central requires an Internet connection.*

Creating loops

Another way of creating a perfect sound track for many Flash animations or videos is the use of an audio clip that loops endlessly. Instead of working with the music you've just customized in the last step, maybe all you need for your project is a loop that you can create by pulling a short section of music out of a longer piece. In Soundbooth, loops are not difficult to create.

About loops

Often a loop of audio is a short section of music, anywhere between 7 to 30 seconds, pulled out of a larger piece. The loop is edited to transition seamlessly from the end back to the beginning, so that by playing repetitions of the loop you can create a virtually endless piece of music, which gives you great flexibility for matching the sound track to your visual work. Loops are generally more successful for short pieces of visual work, otherwise the repetition tends to soon become irritating. A loop is best created from a short piece of music containing a steady tempo, rather than one with ramping moods.

Other than the advantage of matching the length of your visual work exactly, using loops can help to reduce file sizes—which is especially beneficial for multimedia projects such as Flash animations, web sites, video games, or PowerPoint presentations, where you might have to provide a variety of music scores.

Determine the length of a loop

To create a loop from a section of a longer piece of music, you first have to select that section in waveform.

1 Choose File > Open. In the Open Files dialog box, navigate to the Lesson06 folder. Within that folder you will see the file Piano_06.wav—a piano recording from which you will select a small section to create a loop.

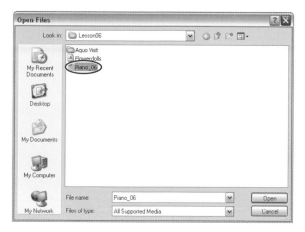

2 In the Open Files dialog box, select the file Piano_06.wav, and then click Open, or simply double-click the file to open its waveform in the Editor panel.

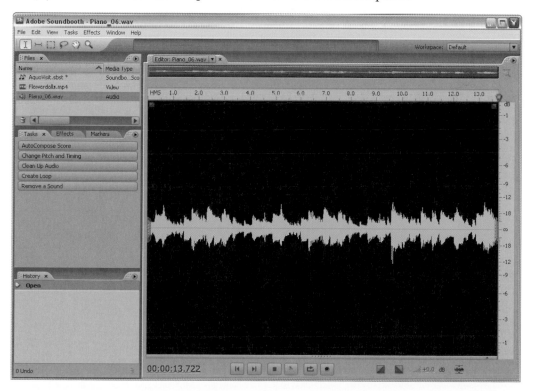

3 Press the spacebar to start playback. The current-time indicator moves from left to right as the piano piece is played for you.

The waveform to be isolated and used as a loop starts at the beginning of the file and ends near the 4.5 second mark. You will first zoom in to get a better view of the waveform near the 4.5 second mark, and then use the Create Loop task to create a loop.

4 With the Zoom tool (🔍) selected, zoom into the area from approximately the 4.4 second mark to the 4.7 second mark of the file.

5 Near the 4.5 second mark (at 00:00:04.551) is a peak in the waveform. Position the current-time indicator at this point in the timeline.

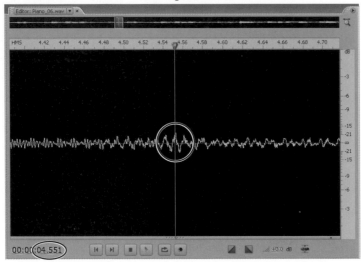

Note: To avoid audible clicks in loop playback, you should aim to set loop in and out points at a zero crossing—where the waveform crosses the zero line. In this exercise, a sub-optimal out point is selected to demonstrate the Auto-Smooth Loop Point option (see next page).

6 In the Tasks panel, click Create Loop, or choose Tasks > Create Loop.

7 In the Create Loop section of the Tasks panel, set the Loop In Point to 00:00:00.000, leaving the Loop Out Point at its current value of 00:00:04.551. Select Lock Duration and choose Play Transition Only.

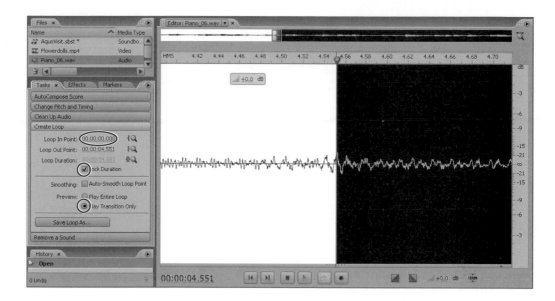

8   Press the spacebar to start playback. If you listen carefully, you will hear a click sound at the point of transition (mainly because you did not select a zero crossing in the waveform as loop out position). In the next step this transition will be smoothed out.

Experience the Auto-Smooth Loop Point option

This feature creates a smoother transition by cross-fading the audio from the out point to the in point.

1   Select the Auto-Smooth Loop Point option, and then listen again. The click sound disappeared and the transition is smooth.

2   Select Play Entire Loop and listen to a few repetitions of the loop you just created. It sounds good, doesn't it?

3   Click the Save Loop As button and save your loop as Piano_06_Loop.wav into your
Lesson06 folder.

4   In the Save As Options dialog box, click OK, accepting the default settings. In
Lesson 9, "Importing, Exporting, and Round-trip Editing," you will learn more about
the different export settings options.

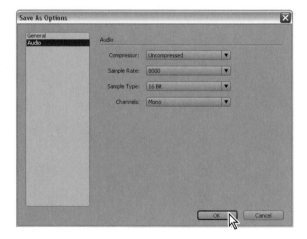

💡 *You can also make video loops from a video file with soundtrack. Once you've created
the loop, just save it in the video file format of your choice.*

Finished! You've now learned different methods of creating and customizing
background music to perfectly fit your work.

Review

▶ ## Review questions

1   What is the AutoComposer?

2   How can you change the overall mood of your score with the AutoComposer?

3   What is a loop?

4   What does the Auto-Smooth Loop Point option do?

Review answers

1   The AutoComposer facilitates the creation of music that matches the mood of visuals through customizing scores derived from a large library of pre-composed score templates.

2   The AutoComposer enables parameters such as intensity or melody to be changed using sliders. Additional adjustable parameters may be available, depending upon the characteristics of the particular score template.

3   A loop is a short piece of music that is edited to transition seamlessly from the end back to the beginning, so that repetitive playing of the loop creates an effectively endless piece of music.

4   The Auto-Smooth Loop Point option enables the creation of smooth transitions at loop boundaries. This is done by cross-fading the audio from the out point of one loop to the in point of the following loop.

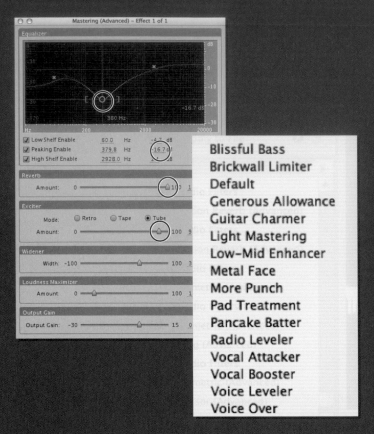

Benefit from a large collection of audio filters—including reverb, echo, EQ, distortion, chorus, and more—that will help you produce the ideal sound track for your project. Apply professionally designed effect presets to get a jump start, and then tweak the settings for the result you are looking for.

7 | Exploring Effects

Effects are used to enhance and modify a waveform to boost the impact of your sound track. Synthesizing, echoing parts, or changing the speed of an audio signal are but a few effects that can add drama, emphasize artistic qualities, and render your work more interesting. Soundbooth offers a wide variety of such effects, ranging from standard effects with a minimal set of options to advanced effects that provide more options to fine-tune to perfection.

In this lesson, you will do the following:

- Look at some key effects.
- Preview and apply an effect.
- Fine-tune a standard effect.
- Delete an effect.
- Set the parameters of an advanced effect.
- Work with the effects rack presets.
- Customize an effects rack preset.

Before you begin, make sure that you have correctly copied the Lessons folder from the CD in the back of this book onto your computer's hard disk. See "Copying the Classroom in a Book files" on page 2.

Getting started

Perform the following steps to ensure that you start the lesson with the default window layout.

1   Start Adobe Soundbooth.

2   Select Window > Workspace > Default, if it is not already selected. Then, choose Window > Workspace > Reset "Default."

3   In the Reset Workspace dialog box, click OK.

Applying a standard effect

In the first part of this lesson, you'll apply a standard effect to parts of your music file.

Previewing an effect

1   Choose File > Open.

2   In the Open Files dialog box that appears, navigate to your Lesson07 folder you copied to your hard disk. Within that folder, select the file Twinkle_Twinkle_07.wav, and then click Open.

3   In the Editor panel, click the Play button (▶) in the group of transport control buttons, or press the spacebar to begin playback. You'll hear a voice recording of the old nursery rhyme, Twinkle, Twinkle, Little Star.

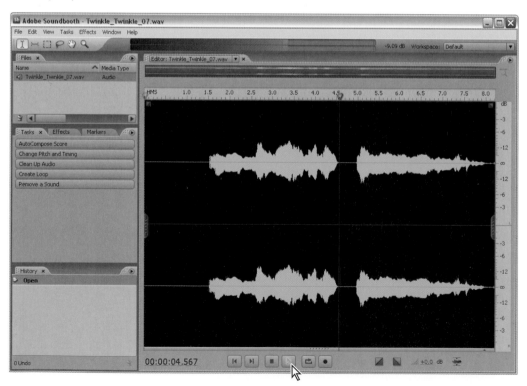

Let's apply an effect to the second part of the recording to compare with the first part, which will remain unchanged.

4   In the Tools panel, select the Time Selection tool (I).

5   In the waveform display, click and drag to select the second half of the waveform, and then release the pointer.

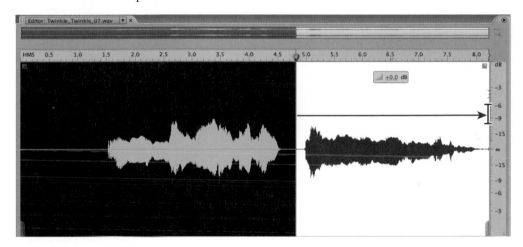

Note: Unless a specific area is selected in the waveform, effects will apply to the entire file.

6   Choose Effects > Convolution Reverb, which creates the impression of space. The Effects panel will come forward, and the Convolution Reverb effect is added to the Effects Rack. The green Power button (⏻) indicates that the effect is on.

 Another quick way of choosing an effect is to right-click (Windows) or Control-click (Mac OS) in the Effects panel, and then choose Convolution Reverb (or any other effect you want to add) from the context menu.

7   From the Effect Preset menu of the Convolution Reverb effect, choose Smeared Beyond Recognition - Aggressive.

8   Click the Play button (▶) to preview the processed audio file.

> 💡 *With the Effect Preset menu in focus (indicated by the blue frame), you can quickly preview the different effect presets by pressing the up or down arrow keys on your keyboard while playing the sound. Make sure to activate Loop Playback (🔁) in the Editor panel.*

It's quite amazing how much more dimensional your sound becomes when this effect is added. You can imagine what different emotional states you might portray by using any of the many other effects. But it's usually best to apply effects sparingly to avoid distracting attention from the intended focus of your work.

Quick effects reference

For most effects, Soundbooth offers both standard and advanced versions. Standard effects provide a compact set of options so that you can quickly optimize sound without detailed audio knowledge. Advanced effects provide a detailed set of options that you can fine-tune to achieve precise sonic results. For more detailed information about the effect settings, refer to Soundbooth Help.

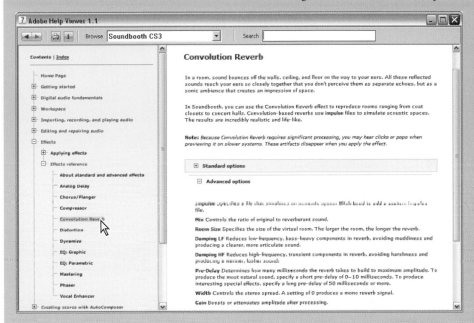

Analog Delay

The Analog Delay effect creates both echoes and other subtle effects. Delays of 35 milliseconds or more create discrete echoes, while delays of 15–35 milliseconds create a simple chorus or flanging effect. Further reducing a delay to 10–15 milliseconds adds stereo depth to a mono sound.

Chorus/Flanger

The Chorus/Flanger effect combines two popular delay-based effects. The Chorus option simulates several voices or instruments played at once by adding multiple short delays with a small amount of feedback. The result is lush, rich sound. Use this effect to enhance vocal tracks or add stereo spaciousness to mono audio.

Compressor

The Compressor effect reduces dynamic range, producing consistent volume levels and increasing perceived loudness. Compression is particularly effective for voiceovers, because it helps the speaker stand out over musical soundtracks and background audio.

(continued on next page.)

Quick effects reference (cont.)

Convolution Reverb

In a room, sound bounces off the walls, ceiling, and floor on the way to your ears. All these reflected sounds reach your ears so closely together that you don't perceive them as separate echoes, but as a sonic ambience that creates an impression of space.

Distortion

Use the Distortion effect to simulate blown car speakers, muffled microphones, or overdriven amplifiers.

Dynamics

The Dynamics effect can be used as a compressor, limiter, and expander. As a compressor and limiter, this effect reduces dynamic range, producing consistent volume levels. As an expander, it increases dynamic range by reducing the level of low-level signals.

EQ: Graphic

The EQ: Graphic effect boosts or cuts specific frequency bands and provides a visual representation of the resulting EQ curve. Unlike the parametric equalizer, the graphic equalizer uses preset frequency bands for quick and easy equalization.

EQ: Parametric

The EQ: Parametric effect provides maximum control over tonal equalization. Unlike the graphic equalizer, which provides a fixed number of frequencies and Q bandwidths, the parametric equalizer gives you total control over frequency, Q, and gain settings.

Mastering

Mastering describes the complete process of optimizing audio files for a particular medium, such as radio, video, CD, or the Web. Before mastering audio, consider the requirements of the destination medium.

Phaser

Similar to flanging, phasing shifts the phase of an audio signal and recombines it with the original, creating psychedelic effects popularized by musicians of the 1960s. But unlike the Flanger effect, which uses variable delays, the Phaser effect sweeps a series of phase-shifting filters to and from an upper frequency. Phasing can dramatically alter the stereo image, creating unearthly sounds.

Vocal Enhancer

The Vocal Enhancer effect quickly improves the quality of voiceover recordings. The Male and Female modes automatically reduce sibilance and plosives, as well as microphone handling noise such as low rumbles. Those modes also apply microphone modeling and compression to give vocals a characteristic radio sound. The Music mode optimizes soundtracks so they better complement a voice-over.

—From Soundbooth Help

Fine-tuning a standard effect

The presets of those standard effects can be modified. In the next steps you will tone down the effect a little.

1   Click Settings next to Convolution Reverb to open the Convolution Reverb Effect options panel.

2   Drag the Amount slider to the left to achieve a value of 50%.

3   Click the Play button ( ) to preview the processed audio file. While playing the audio you can drag the slider from one side to the other to notice the difference. To return to the effects default settings, if needed, click Reset.

> 💡 *To save a preset, choose New Preset from the Effect Preset menu or click the New effect preset button ( ).*

4   Now let's add a second effect that will give the recording a more psychedelic sound. Choose Effects > Phaser to add the effect to the Effects Rack, and then select Over and Under - Moderate from the Effect Preset menu.

Note: For easy access, the last effect you added appears as first item in the Effects menu. To re-create the settings you most recently applied, choose Last Applied Settings from the Effect Preset, or Last Applied Rack from the Rack Preset.

5   Click the Play button ( ) to preview the processed audio file.

Removing an effect

1 To remove the effect you just added, make sure the Phaser effect is still selected in the Effects panel, and then click the Remove selected effects button (🗑) located in the lower right corner of the Effects panel.

💡 *To remove all effects from the Effects Rack, right-click (Windows) or Control-click (Mac OS) in the Effects panel, and then choose Remove All Effects from the context menu.*

Applying effects

So far you've been adjusting and previewing an effect. Only once you apply an effect is the audio processed and the waveform altered. When using the original audio it is generally best to preview and refine effects and effect combinations before applying them, which then permanently alters the waveform.

1 In the Effects panel, click the Apply to Selection button.

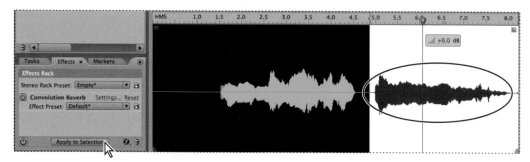

2 All effects in the Effects Rack are processed and the Effects Rack becomes empty. Notice the big change in the waveform after the effect has been applied.

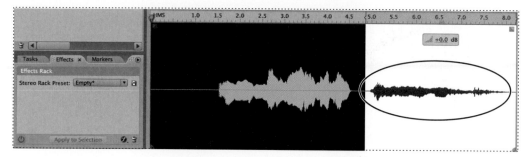

3 As you don't need this standard effect for the next exercise, go to the History panel and click the first entry in the list that reads "Open." One click and you're back where you started, with the original version of the Twinkle, Twinkle waveform in your Editor panel and no effects in your Effects panel.

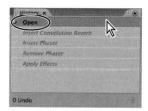

Customizing an advanced effect

Now that you know more about the standard effects, let's have a look at the advanced effects, which have more parameters to fine-tune.

Previewing an advanced effect

Mastering refers to the final optimization of a sound file for the intended output media, as already mentioned in Lesson 5, "Editing and Enhancing Voiceover Recordings." However, some of Soundbooth's Mastering effects are useful to generally improve your audio, or to apply some interesting effects.

1 If necessary, deselect any selection by clicking anywhere in the Editor panel with the Time Selection tool (☐).

2   Choose Effects > Advanced > Mastering (Advanced).

3   From the Mastering (Advanced) Effect Preset menu, choose Dream Sequence.

4   Press the spacebar to preview the audio. The voice now sounds as if coming from far away.

5   Click Settings next to Mastering (Advanced) in the Effects Rack. The Mastering (Advanced) options panel appears, offering a variety of parameters to fine-tune the effect.

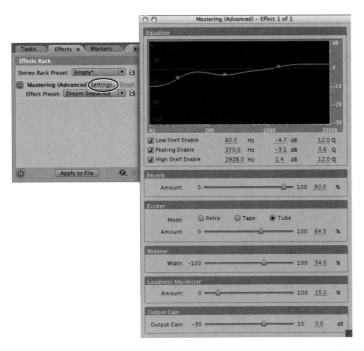

6 The Equalizer enables you to adjust the volume for various frequency bands. Drag the center cross on the red curve downwards to adjust the volume of that band to about -16.7 dB. Alternatively, you can directly edit the blue numbers for the center band called Peaking. Drag the Reverb slider to the full value of 100% to add ambiance. Drag the Exciter slider to a value of 90%. The Exciter exaggerates high-frequency harmonics, adding crispness and clarity.

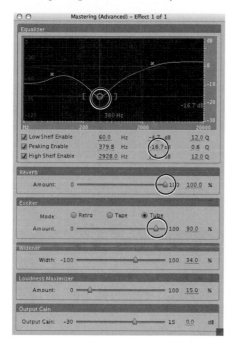

7 Press the spacebar to preview the audio. Notice the difference from the predefined settings before you fine-tuned the effect.

8 Close the Mastering (Advanced) options panel.

This is just one advanced effect. There are endless possibilities to add further effects and really refine your piece to perfection.

Saving a customized effect

Once you're happy with the fine-tuning of your effect, it's a good idea to save your settings and add them to your list of effect presets.

1 To save your current setting as a preset, choose New Preset from the Effect Preset menu, or click the New effect preset button ().

2 In the New Preset dialog box that appears, type **Twinkle** as preset name, and then click OK.

3 Select the Effect Preset menu again and notice within the list the new name you just created.

Deleting an effect preset

In the previous exercise you have saved your customized effect as a preset. It will remain available for your future projects until you decide to delete it from the preset list.

1 To delete the Twinkle preset, make sure it is selected, and then choose Delete Preset from the Effect Preset menu.

2 In the Preset Warning dialog box, click Yes to confirm that you wish to delete the preset "Twinkle."

3 Empty your Effects Rack by selecting the Mastering (Advanced) effect in your Effects panel, and then clicking the Remove selected effects button (⬚).

Working with rack presets

Another easy way to combine or customize effects is to work with rack presets from the Stereo Rack Preset menu when you are working with a stereo recording, or the Mono Rack Preset menu for a mono recording. Soundbooth offers you a wide variety of rack presets that cover the most common sound editing needs. Often those rack presets use more than one effect to achieve optimal results.

Customizing a rack preset

In the next exercise, you will select a rack preset from the Stereo Rack Preset menu and change a parameter. That modified combination of effects and settings will be saved and added to your list of rack presets. You can add up to five effects to the effects rack.

1 From the Stereo Rack Preset menu with its many, many options to select from, choose Voice: Increase Clarity.

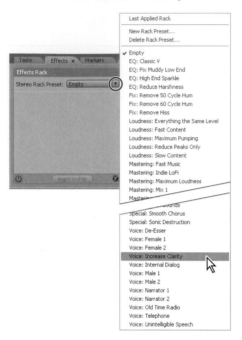

2 Press the spacebar to listen to the audio. This preset combines the EQ: Graphic (Advanced) and the Compressor (Advanced) effects. The clarity of the audio has improved and the voice sounds fuller.

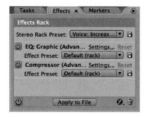

💡 *To bypass a specific effect, click its Power button (⏻). To bypass all effects, click the rack power button in the lower-left corner of the Effects panel.*

3   To fine-tune the effect, choose Voice Thickener in the Effect Preset menu of the Compressor (Advanced) effect.

4   Listen again to the audio by pressing the spacebar.

5   Save these customized settings as a new rack preset by choosing New Rack Preset from the Stereo Rack Preset menu. In the New Rack Preset dialog, enter **Twinkle_2** as rack preset name before clicking OK to close the dialog box.

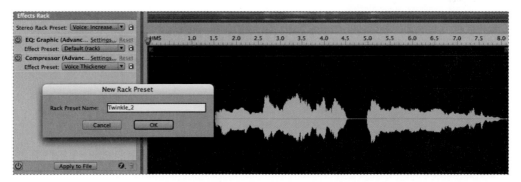

By defining effects rack presets with a common menu name prefix, you can group all your customized presets—using one or multiple effects—in one menu location.

6   Click Apply to File. Notice the change to the waveform in the Editor panel, as well as the effects being cleared from the Effects Rack.

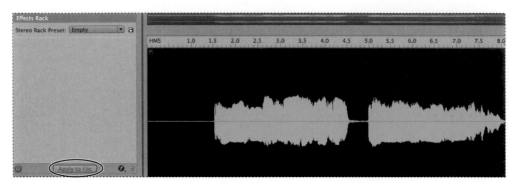

7   Click the Stereo Rack Preset menu. In the list of presets and you will still find the Twinkle_2 preset you have created with the customized parameters. Select Twinkle_2 from the list to make it the current stereo rack preset. The EQ: Graphic (Advanced) and Compressor (Advanced) effects are again added to the effects rack. Notice that Voice Thickener (rack) is selected as effect preset for the Compressor (Advanced) effect, reflecting your modifications before you saved the Twinkle_2 customized rack preset.

Deleting a rack preset

1   With Twinkle_2 as the current Stereo Rack Preset, choose Delete Rack Preset from the Stereo Rack Preset menu. In the Rack Preset Warning dialog box that appears, click Yes to confirm that you wish to delete the rack preset "Twinkle_2."

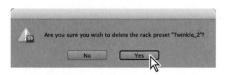

Your Stereo Rack Preset menu is back to its original state.

2   Now might be a good time to check out other presets and experiment with their settings. When you're done, either save you favorite setting for future projects, or close the file without saving.

Congratulations! You've now finished Lesson 7. In doing so, you've been exploring some effect presets as well as effect rack presets. You've tried out standard effects as well as advanced ones, and you customized an effects rack preset. In the next chapter you will learn about markers, which will help you to quickly jump to different sections of your audio or trigger actions in Flash.

Review

Review questions

1 What are sound effects used for?

2 What is the difference between previewing and applying an effect?

3 How do you set the parameters for an effect?

4 What is the effect of changing the Equalizer, Reverb and Exciter parameters in the Mastering (Advanced) effect?

5 How do you customize an effect preset in the Effects Rack?

Review answers

1 Sound effects are artificially created to enhance your audio. Some effects fix problems like poor recording quality by eliminating clicks and pops, while other effects add drama to your audio by creating sounds that are out of the ordinary, or by projecting an impression of space, with echoes and distortions.

2 As long as you only preview an effect, the data in the waveform file is not modified. By applying an effect, all the information relating to the sound effect is included in the waveform and therefore the waveform is altered. It's best to refine an effect by previewing, and then apply the effect as the last step.

3 To set the parameters for an effect, select the effect and then click Settings in the Effects panel.

4 With the Equalizer you can adjust the volume in selected frequency bands. The Reverb parameter adds ambience by giving the impression of space. The Exciter parameter exaggerates high-frequency harmonics, adding crispness and clarity.

5 To customize the settings of an effect preset, open the effect options panel by clicking Settings next to the effects name in the Effects Rack. After modifying the settings, choose New Preset from the Effect Preset menu, or click the New Effect Preset button and provide a new name for the customized effect preset.

With the help of markers you can quickly navigate through your project and jump to specific locations in the file. Additionally, markers can hold information used to synchronize text, sounds, or other interactive elements.

8 | Working with Markers

Markers label important points or sections in your audio. They facilitate navigating within a waveform to make selections, perform editing tasks, or play back audio. As an example, you might consider marking a long recording, or one that has been edited into different scenes, to jump quickly to specific times.

These markers, which can be set millisecond-accurate, can be exported as an XML file for use as cue points in a Flash animation to trigger actions based on audio cues, or to be edited via a text editor. The XML file can also be reimported into Soundbooth and used for a different audio file.

Flash developers who need timing points for subtitles and alternate language support will especially appreciate the ability to add marker data in Soundbooth.

In this lesson, you will do the following:

- Add and delete markers.
- Reposition markers.
- Navigate using markers.
- Edit marker data.
- Export marker data.
- Import marker data into Soundbooth.

Before you begin, make sure that you have correctly copied the Lessons folder from the CD in the back of this book onto your computer's hard disk. See "Copying the Classroom in a Book files" on page 2.

Getting started

Perform the following steps to ensure that you start the lesson with the default window layout.

1 Start Adobe Soundbooth.

2 Select Window > Workspace > Default, if it is not already selected. Then, choose Window > Workspace > Reset "Default."

3 In the Reset Workspace dialog box, click OK.

Working with markers

Adding markers to a sound file is an easy task that can help you to work much more efficiently. To get you started, you will set markers in the piano piece you might recognize from Lesson 4 of this book.

Setting, repositioning, and deleting a marker

1 Choose File > Open, or use the keyboard shortcut, Ctrl+O (Windows) or Command+O (Mac OS).

2 In the Open Files dialog box that appears, navigate to your Lesson08 folder. Within that folder, select the file Solace_08.wav, and then click Open.

3 Select the Zoom tool (🔍) in the Tools panel. In the Editor panel, zoom in on the beginning of the music by clicking there three of four times with the Zoom tool.

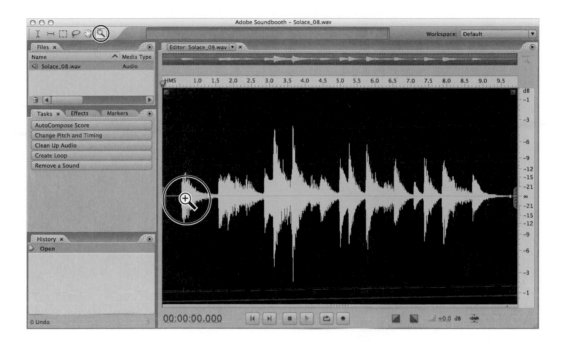

4   Click and drag in the timeline ruler to position the current-time indicator at the beginning of the first waveform, the position for the first marker.

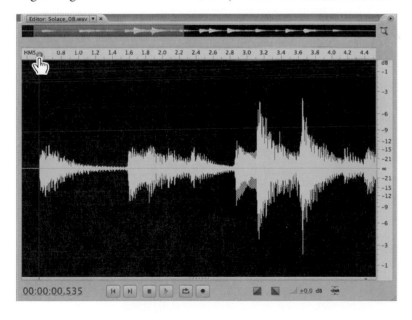

5　You can also position the current-time indicator by clicking the Timecode control, the blue numbers in the lower left corner of the Editor panel, and then entering a time code. We used the value **00:00:00.538**.

6　With the current-time indicator positioned where you would like to set a marker in the Editor panel, click the Add Marker button (✛) in the Markers panel (Window > Markers).

💡 *To add a marker at the position of the current-time indicator, you could also press the keyboard shortcut Shift+8 on a standard keyboard, or press the asterisk (*) key on the numeric key pad, or choose Edit > Marker> Set Flash Cue Point. Markers can also be added while recording: As you record, click the Add Marker button in the Record dialog box to add an audio marker at the current position in the recording.*

7　Notice the newly added small marker icon (🔖) in the timeline ruler.

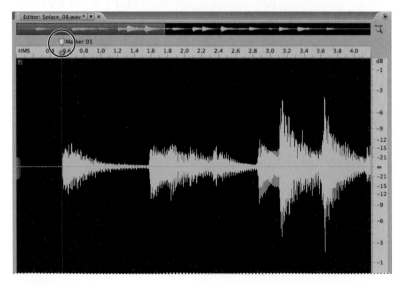

8 Click the Zoom Out Full button () in the upper right corner of the Editor panel to see the entire file.

9 In the same manner as described above, set a second marker at 00:00:04.942 (in the middle of the piece), and a third marker at 00:00:09.755 (near the end of the recording).

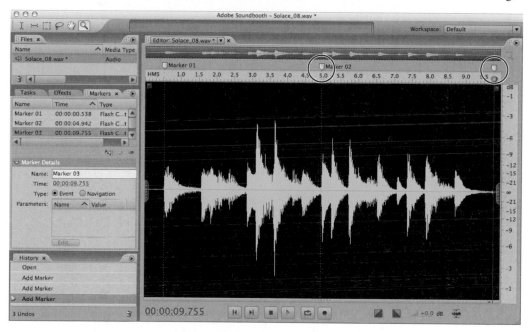

10 To reposition the third marker in the Editor panel, click and drag its marker icon in the timeline ruler.

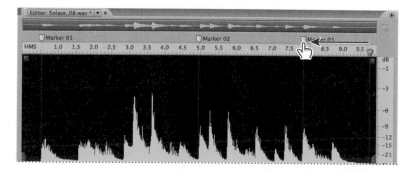

11 To position the third marker at an exact point in time—let's say the 9 second mark—do the following: In the Markers panel, click to select Marker 03 in the list of markers. If necessary, expand the Marker Details section. Double-click the blue number next to Time, and then type the new value of **00:00:09.000** in the text field that appears. Press enter to confirm your entry. Notice in the Editor panel that the third marker has been repositioned to its new location.

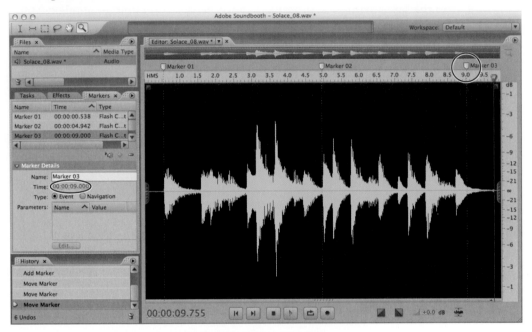

12 As the last step of this exercise, you will delete the third marker. With Marker 03 still selected in the Markers panel, click the Clear Marker button (▬).

You can select multiple markers and delete them all at the same time. To select multiple markers, either drag-select them in the Markers panel, or hold down the Shift or Ctrl/Control key when clicking to select them. Alternatively to using the Clear Marker button, you can right-click (Windows) or Control-click (Mac OS) in the markers list, and then choose Delete Selected Markers from the context menu. To delete all markers, choose Remove All Markers from the context menu, or choose Edit > Marker > Remove All Markers.

Done. Now you know how to set, reposition, and delete markers. Next you will learn how to use those markers to navigate in your file.

Navigating with markers

1   With the current-time indicator still positioned near the end of the file where you deleted the third marker, click the Go To Previous Marker button (◼) at the bottom of the Editor panel. The current-time indicator will jump to the second marker. Click the same button again to jump to the first marker. Use the Go To Next Marker button (◼) to jump from marker to marker in the other direction.

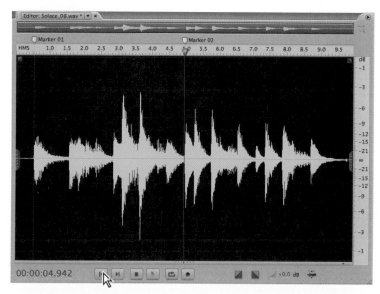

Note: The Go To Previous Marker button and Go To Next Marker button treat the start and end of the file and the start and end of a current selection as implicit markers.

When working with many markers, navigating one step at a time from one marker to the next is not very efficient. In such cases you can use the Markers panel to jump directly to a specific marker.

2   In the Markers panel, double-click the marker you want to jump to. Or, select the marker, and then click the Go To button (you might need to resize the panel to be able to see this button). This will position the current-time indicator at the selected marker in the Editor panel.

💡 *Select the Auto Play button (▣) in the Markers panel to automatically start playback when you go to a marker. This option helps you to quickly identify marker locations.*

Defining marker data for reuse

As you might have already seen in the Markers panel, a marker—called a cue point in Flash—can store more information than just its location. Those details help to identify the sections of the audio, e.g. when a Flash action should be triggered.

Editing marker data

To show Soundbooth's close integration with Flash, in the next exercise we will edit the markers in the Markers panel so that they could be used as cue points in Flash. For this, you need to specify whether the marker is an Event marker or a Navigation marker.

1   Select the first marker in the Markers panel. Notice in the Marker Details section that this marker is an Event marker, the default type when creating new markers. Change the marker type to Navigation marker by clicking the Navigation radio button.

2   Marker parameters consist of name / value pairs. In the Marker Details section, add a new parameter name / value pair by clicking the Add Parameter button (⊕).

3   Type **English title** in the parameter name field, and then enter **Solace first movement** as parameter value. Click OK.

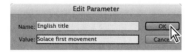

These name / value pairs can later be accessed by an ActionScript in Flash. It's up to the ActionScript programmer—which might or might not be you—how to utilize the information provided.

About marker data

At minimum, a marker defines a specific time within a file. But a marker can also carry additional data like specifying the text of a caption. When working with many markers, it is a good idea to give each marker a unique and descriptive name.

The markers you create in Soundbooth can be loaded as external cue point data in Flash. The data can then be accessed from within an ActionScript or media player application. The advantage of using external marker data is that you can quickly adjust this information. A drawback of using external marker data is that the time of each marker is not essentially linked to a keyframe in your Flash video.

There are two types of marker: Event markers and Navigation markers. You can choose a marker type in the Marker Details panel:

Event Markers

This marker type gets revealed only to ActionScript handlers and can be used to trigger an action, e.g. removal of a title before the next scene title appears. Another use for event markers could be the addition and removal of captions for speech, as those are independent from scene points within a video clip. For further information, see "Learning ActionScript in Flash" at http://www.adobe.com/support/documentation/en/flash.

Navigation Markers

The function of this marker type is to enable you quickly navigate your waveform or projects by jumping from one marker to the next. Whenever the user clicks the next or previous button, playback resumes at the corresponding navigation marker. Note: When streaming a Flash video, you can only jump forward if that portion of the file has already been downloaded.

4 Choose File > Save As. In the Save As dialog box, navigate to your Lessons08 folder, name the file **Solace_marker.wav**, and then click Save.

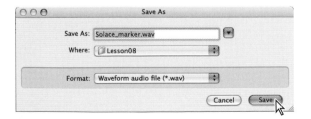

5   In the Save As Options dialog box, accept the default settings by clicking OK.

In Lesson 9, "Importing, Exporting, and Round-trip Editing," you will learn more about file formats and their options in the Save As options dialog box.

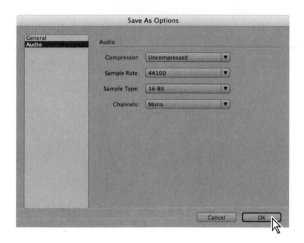

6   If you look into your Lessons08 folder, you will notice a new external file called Solace_marker.wav_markers.xml. This file, containing the information associated with the markers, has been automatically generated when the file Solace_marker.wav was saved.

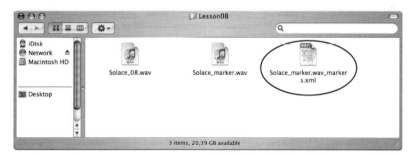

When saving your project in Adobe Flash Video (.flv) format, Flash cue point information will be embedded in the media file.*

Importing marker data into Soundbooth

When next opening the file Solace_marker.wav, Soundbooth would automatically import the associated marker data stored in the file Solace_marker.wav_markers.xml. Soundbooth assumes that any two files stored in the same folder and named *filename* and *filename*_markers.xml are a sound file and its associated marker data.

If you wanted to reuse the marker data within another sound file, you can do so by importing the marker data like parameter names and values.

For this exercise you will import the marker data into the file Solace_08.wav, which—in its original state—had no markers defined.

1   To close the file Solace_marker.wav, select its name in the Files panel, and then click the Close File button (⬚).

2   If necessary, select the file Solace_08.wav as the current file in the Editor panel. Notice that the file does not contain any markers.

3   Select File > Import > Markers.

4   In the Import Markers dialog box, select the file Solace_marker.wav_markers.xml in the Lessons08 folder, and then click Open.

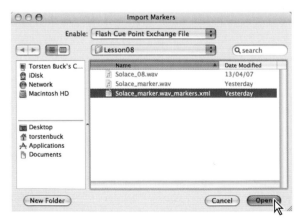

5 The file Solace_08.wav now includes the 2 markers you exported when saving the file Solace_markers.wav.

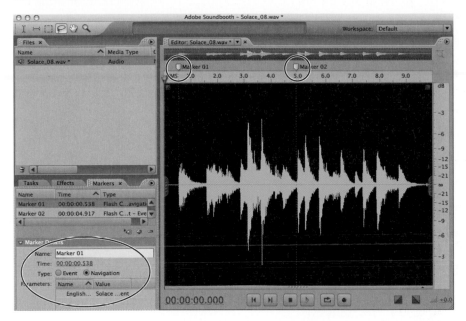

Bravo! You've finished another lesson and you learned about working with markers and how they can help you to navigate your sound files. You've also seen how to set the marker type, add parameters, and export marker data for reuse in other projects.

Review

▶ **Review questions**

1   What is a marker?

2   How can you add a marker?

3   What is the difference between an Event marker and a Navigation marker?

4   What does a file that ends with ._markers.xml generally contain, and in which location would you expect to find it?

▶ **Review answers**

1   A marker, or cue point in Flash, represents a specific point within a waveform. Its data can be used to navigate quickly through a file or to trigger an action. Efficient use of markers can considerably speed up the editing and navigation process.

2   To add a marker, one needs to position the current-time indicator at the specific time to be marked. Then, press Shift+8 or the asterisk (*) key on the numeric pad, or choose Edit > Marker > Set Flash Cue Point, or click the Add Marker button in the Markers panel.

3   While an Event marker gets revealed only by ActionScript handlers and generally triggers an action, such as the appearance of captions, the Navigation marker is predominantly used to travel quickly through the waveform.

4   When saving a file with markers, Soundbooth automatically generates an external file containing the marker data. This file shares the same name as your Soundbooth project, with _markers.xml as an extension, and is saved to the same location as your project file.

Adobe Soundbooth CS3 enables you to import and export files in a wide variety of formats to suit your needs. Tight integration with Adobe Premiere Pro and Adobe AfterEffects enables smooth roundtrip editing.

9 | Importing, Exporting, and Round-trip Editing

Soundbooth can open sound and video files in a variety of file formats, including AIFF, AVI, MP3, MPEG, QuickTime, WAV, and Windows Media. When saving, you can convert your document to a file format most suitable for your target media, ranging from the Web to CD and DVD. In this lesson, you'll learn how to do the following:

- Open files of different file formats.
- Save and export Soundbooth score documents.
- Select export options.
- Save audio and video files in different file formats.
- Export channels to mono files.
- Invoke Soundbooth from other Adobe applications.

Before you begin, make sure that you have correctly copied the Lessons folder from the CD in the back of this book onto your computer's hard disk. See "Copying the Classroom in a Book files" on page 2.

Getting started

Perform the following steps to ensure that you start the lesson with the default window layout.

1   Start Adobe Soundbooth.

2   Select Window > Workspace > Default, if it is not already selected. Then, choose Window > Workspace > Reset "Default."

3   In the Reset Workspace dialog box, click OK.

Importing files

Soundbooth can open files in a wide range of audio and video file formats. In addition, it can read files in the Soundbooth Score Template (*.sbst) and the Soundbooth Score Document (*.sbsc) file formats. To open a file in Soundbooth, you can browse for it using Bridge, drag and drop the file into Soundbooth from Windows Explorer (Windows) or the Finder (Mac OS), use the Open Files dialog box, or launch Soundbooth from within another application such as Adobe Premiere Pro. In the first part of this lesson, you will work with the Open Files dialog box and learn about the various file formats supported.

1 Choose File > Open, and in the Open Files dialog box, navigate to your Lesson09 folder you copied to your hard disk.

2 From the Files of type (Windows) or Enable (Mac OS) menu choose Windows WAVE audio file (*.wav).

3 Notice how only the folder Aquo Visit and the audio file GuitarRiff_Stereo_09.wav remain available for selection in the Open Files dialog box.

4 Choose AVI Movie (*.avi) from the Files of type (Windows) or Enable (Mac OS) menu. Now the video file Flowerdolls.avi is available for selection instead of the audio file GuitarRiff_Stereo_09.wav. Select Soundbooth Score Document (*.sbsc) from the same menu to see the Soundbooth score document MyScoreDocument.sbsc instead of the video file Flowerdolls.avi.

Note: *A Soundbooth Score Document (*.sbsc) is different from a Soundbooth Score Template (*.sbst) file. You can use the template file to create a new, untitled score document. When saving a score document, it contains a reference to the associated template file plus all the parameters you've customized for the document based on the template.*

5 Finally, choose All Supported Media from the Files of type (Windows) or Enable (Mac OS) menu. Select all three documents in the Lesson09 folder by first clicking the topmost document in the list, and then Shift-clicking the last document, and then click Open.

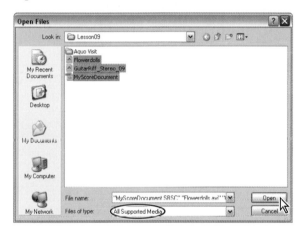

6 If the location of the score template file referenced by the score document has changed since the score document was last saved, you will see the Locate AquoVisit.sbst dialog box. In that case, navigate to the Aquo Visit folder within the Lesson09 folder, select the Soundbooth score template file AquoVisit.sbst, and then click Open.

7 When all three documents have finished opening, notice their different file types under Media Type in the Files panel.

Glossary of audio and video file formats

- **Audio Interchange File Format (.aif)** AIF is the standard, uncompressed audio file format for Mac OS.

- **mp3 Audio (.mp3)** mp3 is the most widely used format for web-based audio and portable media players. This format highly compresses file size, optimizing audio for fast downloads. The compression process, however, slightly reduces quality and introduces artifacts, particularly in quiet passages.

- **Windows Waveform (.wav)** Windows Waveform is the standard audio format for the Windows operating system. By default, WAV files are uncompressed for high audio quality and broad compatibility. However, the Windows version of Soundbooth offers several compression options for specialized applications, such as telephone systems.

- **Adobe Flash Video (.flv)** FLV format lets you present video in Adobe Flash Player, a free, widely available browser plug-in. Adobe Flash Player can play either standalone FLV files, or those you embed into Flash animations in SWF format.

Note: Though Soundbooth can save Adobe Flash Video files, it cannot open them.

- **H.264 (.mp4, .m4v)** Like other variations of MPEG4 format, H.264 offers better compression and lower file size than MPEG2, while maintaining the same perceptual quality. The H.264 codec is supported by the Blu-ray and HD-DVD standards.

- **MPEG1 (.mpg)** The Windows version of Soundbooth supports MPEG-1, a compressed format commonly used on CD-ROM and the web. This format produces picture quality comparable to VHS at quarter-screen frame size.

- **MPEG2 (.mpg, .m2v)** MPEG2 format delivers SVHS picture quality, much higher than MPEG-1. A variation of this format is part of the original DVD specification, but MPEG-2 is also supported by the Blu-ray and HD-DVD standards.

- **QuickTime (.mov)** QuickTime is the standard video format for Mac OS, though its use isn't limited to that platform. However, Windows users must install QuickTime for Windows to view and work with MOV files. In addition to full-resolution video, QuickTime supports streaming video and many different types of compression.

- **RealMedia (.rm)** The Windows version of Soundbooth supports RealMedia, a streaming video format supported by browser plug-ins such as RealPlayer.

Note: Though Soundbooth can save RealMedia files, it cannot open them.

- **Windows Media Video, Windows Media Audio (.wmv, .wma)** The Windows version of Soundbooth supports Windows Media Video and Windows Media Audio, Microsoft's formats for compressed, streaming video and compressed audio, respectively. Typically, WMV and WMA files are played using Windows Media Player, but other applications and plug-ins also support these formats.

> ## Glossary of audio and video file formats (cont.)
>
> • **Microsoft AVI and DV AVI (.avi)** The Windows version of Soundbooth supports two versions of AVI, Microsoft's standard video file format. Regular AVI is uncompressed, retaining all data and high quality. DV AVI uses the DV compression scheme, which is primarily used to exchange video with a DV camera through a FireWire (IEEE 1394) port.
>
> —From Adobe Soundbooth Help

Exporting Soundbooth score documents

When working with Soundbooth score documents it is important to understand the difference between saving a score document and exporting the document's content in an audio or video file format of your choice.

1   If not already selected, choose MyScoreDocument.SBSC from the Files menu in the Editor panel.

This Soundbooth score document was created by customizing the Soundbooth score template file AquoVisit.sbst. It was then saved as a Soundbooth score document (File > Save Soundbooth Score Document As), using MyScoreDocument.SBSC as file name. When opening a saved Soundbooth score document, all customized settings—including referenced clips, if applicable—are instantly restored.

Note: If the file location of the template has changed since you last saved the file, you will be asked to locate it on your hard disk before you can open the file. If the file location of the reference clip has changed, you will see an Open File Failure dialog box. In that case, click OK to close the dialog box, locate and add the reference video to the Files panel, and then select it again from the Reference Clip menu in the AutoCompose Score section of the Tasks panel. Choose File > Save Soundbooth Score Document to save the changes.

Installed score templates

During software installation, 40 Soundbooth score templates are placed in the application folder. These score template (.sbst) files can be previewed and opened in Adobe Bridge, or opened directly from the File menu. Each template was produced by an expert musician, adding professional polish to your projects.

To view installed score templates, navigate to the following folder on your computer:

- **Windows:** *[startup drive]*/Program files/Adobe/Adobe Soundbooth CS3
- **Mac OS:** *[startup drive]*/Applications/Adobe Soundbooth CS3

—From Adobe Soundbooth Help

2   To export your score as an audio or video file, choose File > Export > Soundbooth Score, or click the Export Score button in the AutoCompose Score section of the Tasks panel.

To include audio from the reference clip in the exported file, select the Include Reference Clip Audio Track *check box in the Autocompose Score section of the Tasks panel before exporting the file.*

3   In the Export Soundbooth Score dialog box, notice the choice of available output file formats in the Save as type (Windows) or Format (Mac OS) menu.

Note: Microsoft AVI (*.avi), Microsoft DV AVI (*.avi), MPEG1 (*.mpg), MPEG1-VCD (*.mpg), MPEG2-SVCD (*.mpg), RealMedia (*.rm), Windows Media Video (*.wmv), and Windows Media Audio (*.wma) are only available as output file formats in the Windows version of Soundbooth.

After clicking Save in the Export Soundbooth Score dialog box, you can specify output file format options in either the Save As Options dialog box, the Export Settings dialog box, or the MP3 Compression Options dialog box, depending on the output file format you choose:

• When saving in Audio Interchange File Format (*.aif), QuickTime (*.mov), Microsoft AVI (*.avi), Microsoft DV AVI (*.avi), or Windows Waveform (*.wav) format, the Save As Options dialog box appears with options available in the General, Audio, and—if applicable—Video sections of the dialog box. For in-depth information on the various options available, search for "AIF, AVI, MOV, and WAV options" in Soundbooth Help.

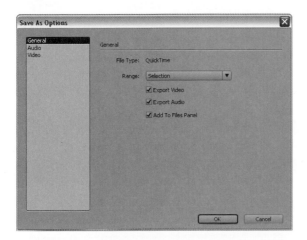

* When saving in MP3 Audio (*.mp3) format, the MP3 Compression Options dialog box appears. For in-depth information on the options available, search for "mp3 options" in Soundbooth Help.

* When saving in Adobe Flash Video (*.flv), H.264 (*.mp4), H.264 Blu-ray (*.m4v), MPEG1 (*.mpg), MPEG1-VCD (*.mpg), MPEG2 (*.mpg), MPEG2-SVCD (*.mpg), MPEG2-DVD (*.m2v), MPEG2 Blu-ray (*.m2v), RealMedia (*.rm), Windows Media Video (*.wmv), or Windows Media Audio (*.wma) format, the Export Settings dialog box appears. For in-depth information on the various options available, search for "Options for additional video formats" in Soundbooth Help.

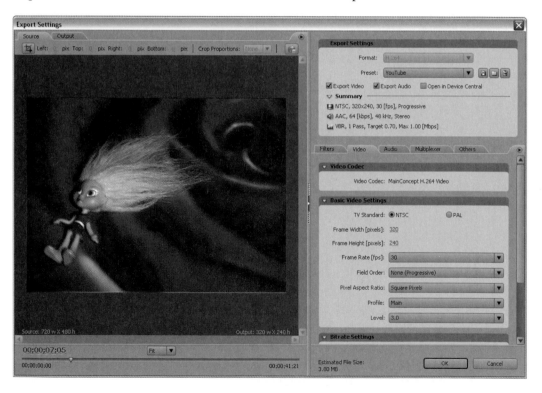

Using export settings presets

The many options available in the Export Settings dialog box can appear overwhelming at first. To simplify things, Soundbooth ships with numerous presets already defined for each output format. All you have to do is select a preset that best matches your output goals to automatically activate the appropriate options in the various setting panels. If necessary, you can then further adjust the settings, and save your changes as a new preset.

1   In the Export Soundbooth Score dialog box, select H.264 (*.mp4) as file format from the Save as type (Windows) or Format (Mac OS) menu, and then click Save.

2   In the Export Settings dialog box, select YouTube from the Preset menu located under Export Settings on the right side of the dialog box.

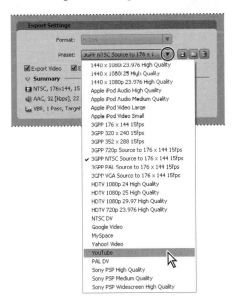

3   By selecting the tabs on the right side of the dialog box you can review and customize the various output option settings used for this preset.

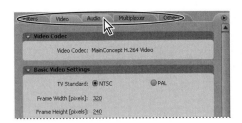

4 Click to select the Output tab on the left side of the Export Settings dialog box. Drag the slider below the large image area to the right to scroll through the movie. Select 100% from the View Zoom Level menu to preview the movie in its final size.

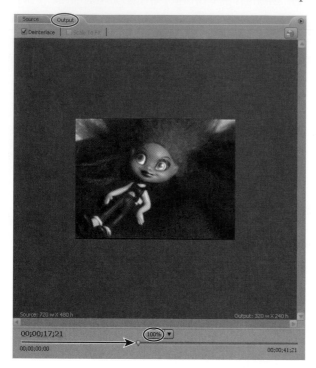

5 To actually export the movie and close the Export Settings dialog box when you are done with adjusting the output settings, you would click OK. Rendering time would depend on the file length, the selected encoding options, and your hardware. For now, just click Cancel to close the Export Settings dialog box without saving any file.

Search for "Options for additional video formats" in Soundbooth Help for detailed information on all the options available in the Export Settings dialog box.

Exporting audio and video files

If the current file in the Editor panel is not a Soundbooth score document, you'll use the Save As dialog box to specify export option settings.

1   In the Editor panel, choose Flowerdolls.avi from the Files menu.

2   To export this file—or any other file that is not a score document—as an audio or video file, choose File > Save As. The Save As dialog box will appear. Notice that this dialog box is—apart from its name—identical to the Export Soundbooth Score dialog box you've just worked with in the previous exercise. If you click Save, you would specify output file format options in either the Save As Options dialog box, the Export Settings dialog box, or the MP3 Compression Options dialog box, depending on the output file format you choose. But for now, just click Cancel.

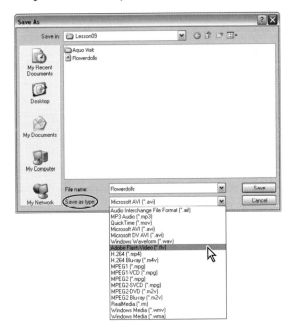

💡 *Use File > Save Selection As to export a currently selected range of the file as an audio or video file.*

Exporting channels to mono files

Another form of exporting is to split a multichannel audio file into separate files—one file for each channel.

1   In the Editor panel, choose GuitarRiff_Stereo_09.wav from the Files menu.

2   Choose File > Export > Channels To Mono Files.

3   In the Browse For Folder (Windows) or Choose Folder for Exported Files (Mac OS) dialog box, select the Lesson09 folder, and then click OK (Windows) or Choose (Mac OS).

Because this file was recorded in stereo, Soundbooth will create two files in the Lesson09 folder, called GuitarRiff_Stereo_09_L.wav for the left channel and GuitarRiff_Stereo_09_R.wav for the right channel. Soundbooth also automatically opens the files so you can start editing the individual channels right away.

Note: *For a file in 5.1 surround-sound format, Soundbooth would create six files in total, named [filename]_L for the left channel, [filename]_R for the right channel, [filename]_Ls for the left surround channel, [filename]_Rs for the right surround channel, [filename]_C for the center channel, and [filename]_LFE for the low-frequency effects channel, respectively.*

Round-trip editing

One of the key features of Soundbooth is its tight integration with Adobe Premiere Pro and Adobe After Effects. These programs feature a menu command to open an audio clip asset in Soundbooth's Editor panel. When you're done with repairing and enhancing the clip, save your changes and the updated audio automatically appears in your video project.

A typical workflow would look as follows:

*   In Adobe Premiere Pro or Adobe After Effects, select an audio-only master clip, subclip, or clip instance in a timeline, and then choose Edit > Edit in Adobe Soundbooth > Edit Source File.

*   Edit the sound file in Soundbooth and save the changes when done.

*   The original file on disk is overwritten and all instances of the master clip, its subclips and track items are updated automatically to reflect the changes.

Note: *The changes cannot be undone.*

> To generate a new project item and leave the original master clip preserved in the project and on disk, select an audio-only or A/V master clip, subclip, or clip instance in a timeline, and choose Edit > Edit in Soundbooth > Extract Audio.

Congratulations! You've completed the last lesson of this book. In doing so, you learned about Soundbooth's supported file formats for import and export, the difference between Soundbooth score documents and other documents when it comes to saving and exporting them, using export settings presets in the Export Settings dialog box, and what a typical round-trip editing workflow would look like when using Soundbooth together with Adobe Premiere Pro or Adobe After Effects. The last thing remaining to do now is to go through the review questions and answers on the next page.

Review

▶ **Review questions**

1   Which command do you use to save a Soundbooth score document in the Soundbooth score document format (*.sbsc)?

2   Which command do you use to export a Soundbooth score document as a video or audio file in a different format?

3   How do you specify output file format options?

4   Describe the round-trip editing workflow between Adobe Premiere Pro or Adobe After Effects and Soundbooth.

▶ **Review answers**

1   When working with Soundbooth score documents, use the File > Save Soundbooth Score Document and File > Save Soundbooth Score Document As commands to save the file in the Soundbooth score document format (*.sbsc). The Soundbooth score document contains references to the score template (and the reference video clip), as well as the parameter settings for the customized score.

2   When working with Soundbooth score documents, use the Export > Soundbooth Score command to export the video and/or audio content of the score in one of the many available output file formats.

3   After clicking Save in the Save As (or the Export Soundbooth Score) dialog box, you can specify output file format options in either the Save As Options dialog box, the Export Settings dialog box, or the MP3 Compression Options dialog box, depending on the output file format you choose.

4   Select an asset in Adobe Premiere Pro or Adobe After Effects and use a menu command to open it in the Soundbooth Editor panel. Edit the asset and save your changes in Soundbooth. The updated audio automatically appears in your video project.

Index

Production Notes

The *Adobe Soundbooth CS3 Classroom in a Book* was created electronically using Adobe InDesign CS2. Additional art was produced using Adobe Illustrator CS2, and Adobe Photoshop CS2.

Team credits

The following individuals contributed to the development of the lessons for this edition of the *Adobe Soundbooth CS3 Classroom in a Book:*

Project coordinators, technical writers: Torsten Buck & Katrin Straub

Production: Manneken Pis Productions (www.manneken.com)

Copyediting & Proofreading: Ross Evans

Designer: Katrin Straub

Special thanks to Christine Yarrow.

Typefaces used

Set in the Adobe Minion Pro and Adobe Myriad Pro OpenType families of typefaces. More information about OpenType and Adobe fonts is available at Adobe.com.

Project Credits

Video and sound files supplied by Katrin Straub, Torsten Buck, and Adobe Systems Incorporated. Those files are for use only with the lessons in the book.